C0-DUQ-163

VISITS WITH MRS. PICKET

"Over the Picket Fence"
author Ruth Guppy's reflections
on Hood River area history, humans
and happenings

— ☙ —

Edited by
Macy Guppy

Excerpts from Ruth Guppy's columns and the
"Panorama"©1951-1991 Hood River News
All rights reserved

All other material © 2012 Macy Guppy
All rights reserved

Published by
Lightning Source Inc.
La Vergne, Tennessee
ISBN 9-780615-68078

October 2012

Cover art: Becki Trachsel-Hesedahl painted the book cover, "Mrs. Picket's Fence," featuring the fence that graced Ruth and Russ's front yard for 35 years and the iris that Ruth so loved. Visit Becki's website at www.redwallstudioarts.net.

DEDICATION

To Dad, whose desire to honor Mom and her love for writing,
history and Hood River inspired "Visits With Mrs. Picket"

— CR —

ACKNOWLEDGMENTS

This book could only become real with generous help from the following people, who gave countless hours of their time and invaluable resources:

The casually organized but very enthusiastic "Visits With Mrs. Picket" editorial board members all knew and appreciated Ruth and her writing. Members include Ruth's niece Elizabeth Berry; former "Hood River News" editor Wally Eakin; Mid-Columbia broadcaster and writer Rodger Nichols; and local columnist Maija Yasui. They provided thoughtful feedback on the book's content.

The History Museum of Hood River County provided much-appreciated financial and research help to bring this book to the larger community.

The "Hood River News" editor, Kirby Neumann-Rea, and staff provided complete access to the newspaper's archives, and Trisha Walker transcribed several of Ruth's columns and articles.

John Krussow generously entrusted me with the notebooks of Ruth's historical research and published articles she had given to John's wife, Pat. Ruth considered Pat a consummate researcher and writer.

Chris and Carolyn Guppy provided valuable feedback and financial assistance with this book.

Malea Guppy transcribed many of the articles in this book and encouraged her mom throughout the project.

Hilary Russell provided exceptional proofreading and — along with Peg Cross and Ann Snyder — made helpful editorial suggestions.

My work colleagues and great friends provided much-needed support and ideas.

Finally, a huge hug and thank you go to artist and graphic designer Becki Trachsel-Hesedahl, co-creator of this beautiful book.

— ∞ —

INTRODUCTION

Ruth McClain Guppy captured the beauty, people and history of the Columbia Gorge area for almost 40 years through her light and breezy "Over the Picket Fence" column and longer historical articles. She filled more than a dozen three-ring binders with her work and placed them on a library shelf in her Hood River home surrounded by the iconic picket fence. The notebooks became a treasure trove for area writers and historians who followed her.

This prolific and gifted writer only had one regret: that she didn't write "her book." She imagined it as a legacy of stories with the historical depth and human quips that were her specialty. Ruth wrote first drafts of a few chapters but, somehow, work and family intervened.

Ruth's book finally comes to life in "Visits With Mrs. Picket" — a collection of her stories and poems published to honor her longtime wish on the 10th anniversary of her death.

Fellow Hood River columnist Maija Yasui sees Ruth's writings as "our link to the history of this valley and all the wisdom provided therein. Ruth was an insightful writer and a passionate environmentalist, long before Rachel Carson penned 'The Silent Spring.'"

Ruth McClain attended the University of Oregon Journalism School during the Great Depression. Although her college fund evaporated when the banks collapsed, Ruth was determined to finish college. That meant a steady diet of five-cent coffees and five-cent hamburgers. Ruth's oldest granddaughter, Carie, remembers childhood visits to her grandparents when she woke up early to the "tap, tap, tap" of her grandmother's typewriter. She considers her "Magee" a pioneer in pushing through educational and professional barriers for women in the 1930s. Carie says Magee's example provided much of the drive she needed to work three jobs during college and veterinary school.

Ruth's diligence paid off. She was one of the top journalism students at a time when women were only beginning to enter the field. Ruth won a slew of academic and writing awards, competing against U of O journalism students such as Tom McCall and Dick Neuberger.

After graduation, Ruth began her writing career as a reporter and then an advertising copywriter. Her curious nature took her to several cities in the western United States where she wrote ad copy for major department stores.

Ruth met Russ Guppy, her husband for 60 years, when they both worked at Seattle's Bon Marché.

When Ruth and Russ were engaged and visited her home town, Russ had the same reaction that Ruth's father had had 30 years earlier: On both men's first view of the pristine Hood River setting, they decided to move their families there. Like her mother, Ruth found her life taking an unexpected turn.

Instead of writing ads, Ruth turned her talents to capturing the Mid-Columbia area's history and to relating snippets of its life. Her busy mind reflected on current events and universal truths through her column, which was published in the "Hood River News" and its predecessor, "The Hood River Daily Sun."

While raising her children, Ruth helped Russ with his business. But writing was always central to her being. Ruth typically rose at 4 a.m. to enjoy the solace for research and writing. A few of those early mornings were punctuated by the sound of a BB gun as Ruth warded off predators lurking around her precious wild birds. Her love of birds and the abundant natural surroundings resonated in her columns and poetry.

"Visits With Mrs. Picket" will give those unfamiliar with Ruth's work a chance to lean over that picket fence and capture her homespun account of the Hood River Valley's people, history and geography.

Those who knew her will revisit Ruth over that same fence and relive the memories through Ruth's prolific pen.

Best of all, Ruth finally has her book to be enjoyed by another generation of Hood Riverites.

— CR —

EDITOR'S NOTES ON
RUTH'S WRITING STYLE

Ruth's many interests cut a wide swath — from bird watching to painting, genealogy to rock identification, handwriting analysis to historical research.

Her abundant interests informed her writing, as did a diverse group of authors such as E.B. White, M.L.K. Fisher and William Safire. She chuckled at Ogden Nash and marveled at Japanese Haiku poets.

The curiosity that kindled Ruth's many interests and her wide-ranging reading came to the fore in her "Over the Picket Fence" column that offered something for everyone. Ruth described its style as inclining toward the type "San Francisco Examiner" writer Herb Caen called the "scattershot" column … short items on a variety of subjects.

She said, "Caen describes it thus: ' … you shoot about 20 arrows into the air … and hope that at least one will hit the reader as he skims through it, sniffing anxiously for a name he recognizes, a place he knows about, or a situation he is mildly interested in.'"

Shooting those arrows became Ruth's gift to the local area. Her lifetime love of words often surfaced in her column. For example, she never met an exclamation point she didn't like. In 1956, when reminded by a reader that some writing authorities say the exclamation point isn't necessary, Ruth replied, "Personally, we couldn't live without the little rascal. It is to writing what the raised eyebrow, the tongue-in-cheek or the hearty laugh are to conversation. So dash off a couple for us, Homer ! ! ! !" [Homer was the "Hood River News" linotype operator at that time.]

Ruth's many years in newsrooms gave her great sympathy for linotype operators', reporters' and editors' perils. Until the late 1960s when I worked at the "Hood River News," Homer and his successors set type with hot lead. Mistakes were easy to make and hard to correct. Ruth unmasked typos' real culprit to News readers in a Sept. 9, 1955 column:

> Has anyone lived whose items appeared in a newspaper exactly and typographically as written! It's doubtful! This is

not to cast aspersions on the staff ... the linotype operators are experts, the proofreaders are beyond reproach!

But every once in awhile a linotype machine burps "is" instead of "as" or "he" when it should be "she" or uncaps a Capital letter, or throws in an extra comma. All this is thanks to little Eteon Schrudel, that naughty gremlin in every newspaper office who loves to gum up the works.

All of which is merely to remind readers, on behalf of editors, reporters, correspondents and columnists, that none of us is as dumb as we sometimes read. Eteon Schrudel is the guy to blame.

This is not to say that Ruth didn't cringe when she spotted a typo after her stories went to press. She clipped each one of her hundreds of columns and historical articles after they were published. Whenever she found a disjointed word or, worst of all, a misspelled name, she corrected it with her proverbial pencil before filing the story away in one of her neat binders.

Of this obsession, she remarked, "Old proofreaders will never get into heaven. We'll all be standing outside the pearly gates proofreading St. Peter's list of names."

In the early years of her writing, Ruth referred to herself as "we" in her columns. But as her confidence grew, she came to question her use of that pronoun. In a 1970 OPF column titled "On My Own," Ruth wrote this:

> There is a certain degree of cowardice in using "we" in a column like this. Who am I trying to involve in the responsibility for what I say when I use the personal pronoun "we"? The Hood River News? No sir! The paper takes no blame nor shares any complicity. I'm on my own.
>
> When I admit to ignorance, writing "we didn't know that!" am I blaming my teachers? When I write that "we" enjoyed a lovely sunrise, who do I mean, my dog and I? Well, usually, yes!
>
> Back in 1952 when this column began, it was anonymously written and then there was no attempt to hide behind "we,"

(continued)

"us," "ours." With the addition of a byline, self-consciousness set in, the column lost a lot of its spontaneity and began hiding its ignorance, foibles and personal opinion behind the righteous shield of "we."

Speaking to those who try to write personal columns, Rudolf Fresch defended the use of "I" and asked, "Can you train yourself to sacrifice your pride and admit all your mistakes and faults and shortcomings, your ignorance, your weakness, your poverty, your irresponsibility?"

Then, for heaven's sake, he added, be honest. Use the first person singular "I" and don't hide behind "we's" skirts.

As times changed, so did writing conventions. The stories in this book are true to Ruth's particular style and those evolving conventions. Her stories appear here just as they were originally published. However, I have added headlines where none appeared in the original articles.

Her stories and poems are divided into topical chapters and arranged chronologically within each topic. You will find the publication date at the end of each column, with some columns including more than one story. Many of her poems, which did not include publication dates or were unpublished, are grouped at the end of some of the chapters.

As a writer, I have been privileged to collect some of Ruth's gems for you. In the process, I learned yet again Ruth's subtle lessons in great writing.

As her daughter, this book's journey has deepened my appreciation of my mom's engaging personality, her love of the place where my brother and I also grew up, and her challenging intellect that drove her throughout her life to understand and discuss the issues of her day. She was perennially curious. In fact, she often said, "I can't die today. I've got something else to learn."

And so it was.

Macy E. Guppy, Ph.D.

— ℭ —

EDITOR'S BIO

Macy is the younger of Russ and Ruth Guppy's two children. She and her brother, Chris, grew up in Hood River and will always treasure their memories of the town and its people. Macy learned to love writing and relish creativity from her mother.

After college, Macy worked in the Midwest, in the Washington, D.C. area and on a remote island in the South Atlantic Ocean. Like her mom, she loved experiencing new places and people but was happy to return to Oregon and settle in Portland.

Macy has been a public relations practitioner, writer and editor for 30 years.

She literally walked the same paths her mother walked when Macy returned to the University of Oregon to pursue her doctorate in communications from the School of Journalism and Communication. Macy studied in some of the same classrooms that Ruth attended 60 years before her. Macy's daughter, Malea, is continuing the family tradition as a U of O student.

— ◌ɹ —

TABLE OF CONTENTS

CHAPTER 1: IT HAPPENED LIKE THIS

— HISTORY OF PLACES, PEOPLE, THINGS

(continued)

CHAPTER 2: GORGE TREASURES
— SNIPPETS OF AREA INTEREST

CHAPTER 3: BIRDS OF A FEATHER

— AND OTHER FASCINATIONS OF NATURE

CHAPTER 4: LOCALS AND NOTABLES
— FAMOUS AND FASCINATING FOLKS

CHAPTER 5: SIGNS OF THE TIMES
— A WISE WOMAN COMMENTS ON SOCIETY AND POLITICS

(continued)

Chapter 5 — continued

CHAPTER 6: HOLIDAYS, SCHMOLIDAYS
— REMEMBERING THE SPECIAL TIMES

(continued)

CHAPTER 7: AROUND THE HEARTH
— FAMILY AND HOME MEMORIES

CHAPTER 8: GRINS, GIGGLES AND GUFFAWS
— HOOD RIVER HUMOR

(continued)

Chapter 8 — continued

— ☙ —

CHAPTER 1

IT HAPPENED LIKE THIS

— History of places, people, things

Long Winter Roundtrip

When inconvenient snow makes it a little difficult to maneuver the car around town, I'm reminded of a lady that tells about life in the early days. From Willow Flat, they came to winter parties in HR by bobsled, and the sun was up when the horses drew into their yard again. Did it often, too. And almost every Saturday in the year they came into town for the weekly shopping starting out in the buggy at 9 a.m., arriving back home by suppertime!

Dec. 31, 1952, Hood River Daily Sun

— ଔ —

Largest Apple Orchard

Interesting if immaterial … Dufur once lay claim to the "largest single apple orchard in the world." The Dufur Orchard Co. owned a 4,000-acre tract, planted in 1911–12. It produced bumper crops of Newtowns, Jonathans, Winter Bananas, Spitzenburgs and Blackstems.

In 1921, 194 railroad cars of apples were taken off the acreage. In 1922 the crop was 125,000 boxes. It took 125 regular workers to handle the orchard, 400 at harvest time and 94 horses.

Despite the huge crops, the orchard was too large to be handled efficiently under existing methods, so in 1922 it went into receivership and was later profitably planted back to wheat.

March 5, 1954

— ଔ —

Prank on the City

Before electric street lighting, the city fathers passed a law stating that everyone on the streets after 6 p.m. should carry a lantern.

(continued)

Well, Bert Stranahan and some of the boys around the livery stable at Front and Oak, always great hands to entertain the town, had the answer to that one. Citizens appeared on the streets with lanterns, all right, but the lanterns weren't lit!

A hasty meeting of the fathers inserted the word "lighted" into the new amendment and everyone had a good laugh.

April 30, 1954

— CR —

AIRFIELD OF OLD

You know where the county gravel pit now is? Well, not too many years ago it was Hood River's airfield, our pride and joy. When a bi-plane warmed up out there, you could hear it all over town. And if you were young, you could start running toward the field from most any point in Hood River and arrive before the plane was off the ground!

FROM WOODS TO COURTHOUSE

The new courthouse is a big change, too, for all those folks in the valley who went to the little old school house which stood on the site. A friend tells us that, as a little girl, she was not allowed to walk alone from school to her home near 13th and State because of the woods! Instead, she waited at the Prather home across from the present library for someone to escort her the rest of the way through the big trees.

FOOTNOTES ON FAMILIAR SCENES

Bingen, Wash., was named for Bingen-on-the-Rhine. So you who call it Bing-en are fully justified.

Billy Sunday, "Mr. Evangelist" himself, bought his ranch south of the present Neal creek mill in 1909. Grew grain and bred fine cattle there. "Ma" Sunday was as colorful and dynamic as her famous husband!

Wyeth was named for Nathaniel Wyeth, who came through the gorge in 1832.

That white shaft you may have seen on Memaloose island east of Mosier was erected in memory of Vic Trevitt, a Dalles pioneer who chose to be buried in the Indian "place of the dead." He said he wanted to sleep among honest people!

May 21, 1954

— ✠ —

No Highway 84 for pioneers

As we whiz west on the highway, irritated at slowing to 35 mph through Cascade Locks, we ought to give a thought to the earliest pioneers as they made their way over this same ground in negotiating the portage around the Cascades.

Since the cross-country wagons were unable to leave the middle west before spring, it was usually November or early the next year before they were ready to challenge the Columbia gorge on rafts.

Said one pioneer woman about the portage walk around the Cascades which was five miles,

> I carry my babe and lead, or rather carry, another through the snow, mud and water almost to my knees.
>
> … I was afraid to look behind me for fear of seeing the wagons turn over in the mud. My children gave out with cold and fatigue …. We started at sunrise and did not get to camp near the present site of Bonneville dam until after dark, and there was not a dry thread on one of us — not even my babe.

Hood River day travel

Speaking of travel, early Parkdale residents recall that, to get to Hood River, they had to ride or walk through dense forests to Dee,

(continued)

take the train to HR, stay overnight and return home the next day. A long jaunt just to go to town!

Feb. 18, 1955

— CR —

1894: POPULATION 350

From an Oregonian handbook of 1894, this condensed picture of Hood River: Present population, 350 … two church buildings, Congregational and United Brethren … school with 80 pupils and two teachers … one dozen stores, two hotels, two livery stables … returns from the 1892 strawberry crop, sold in Montana and Portland, $23,000. Mount Hood may be reached by an easy stage ride of but 28 miles.

April 8, 1955

— CR —

ORTLEY BOONDOGGLE

Probably one of the most fantastic real estate flops in the West occurred only a few miles from Hood River. Ever hear of Ortley?

Laid out nine miles west of The Dalles on the old state road to Mosier, Ortley was to be a cooperative community. The Hood River Orchard and Land Co. acquired 700 acres in 1911, platted a town and laid out the acreage in 5 and 10-acre tracts. These were planted to Ortley apples and sold for $1,700 and up to greenhorns and "gentlemen farmers." The general idea was that the owners could live in the city far away and farm by remote control!

The company was said to have put $200,000 into the unique venture, building a community store and post office, hotel, company house for laborers, school and blacksmith shop.

However, several important items were overlooked. The land was too dry in summer, too wet in winter and too windy even for apples. Bankruptcy, following lawsuits by investors against the company, ended the project in 1919.

You can drive from Mosier to Ortley these Spring days, where the land is cleared for wheat but mainly supports wild larkspur, sunflowers and lupine and, if you are lucky, you may find a few weathered boards as a monument to a $200,000 dream!

May 6, 1955

—◌—

INDIAN MARTHA'S SAD STORY

One of Hood River's most tragic early stories is told of Indian Martha, a familiar figure to long-time residents. Martha was rowing across the Columbia with her two young children when the boat was swamped in the wake of a passing sternwheeler. Either no one aboard noticed or cared to help the Indian woman. With superhuman strength she kept both babies afloat, only to find them dead when she stumbled to shore.

Since there has been some doubt cast upon the veracity of this story, we asked Miss Ella May Davidson about it several years ago. Miss Davidson knew the Indian woman well, because Martha often walked from her cabin above Koberg's beach to the Hood River hotel to get breadcrumbs for her chickens.

Yes, said Miss Davidson, she had once asked Martha about the tragedy and the old Indian replied, putting her hand over her heart, "no talk. Too much hurt here."

Sept. 16, 1955

—◌—

POINT-OF-VIEW RESEARCH

If you find some slight variances in the anniversary edition's early-day history, please remember that much of the material was gathered, not from written records, but by word of mouth, from

(continued)

stories handed down and from fading memories. Thus obtained, seldom are two versions alike.

For example, following our recounting in this column of the tragedy of Indian Martha and her children in the Columbia river, we received two more versions, quite different. One was from the remembered words of a passenger aboard the steamer, the other from a relative of a man who was called to the river after Martha dragged her dead children ashore. In all, this makes five varied stories of the incident for our notebook.

Dec. 16, 1955

— CR —

HOOD RIVER COUNTY JUST 100 YEARS AGO, PART 1

The name changes

The gamey stream fed by Mount Hood glaciers and lakes was called the Labeasche river by Lewis and Clark on Tuesday, October 29, 1805, when they first spotted it where it flowed into the Columbia. This was an improvision on the name of a French-Canadian waterman in their party, Francis Labische.

Later, when a band of cattle was being driven over the trail from The Dalles, it arrived late one evening at the river. The cattle were driven across while the party camped on the east shore. During the night a heavy rainstorm came up and by morning the stream was too high to cross.

It rained for days as the river grew wilder. Food ran out. Finally Old Towser, a dog who had improvidently followed the party, succumbed to the dinner pot. Thus the stream became Dog river and the name clung even long after Mrs. Nathaniel Coe, wife of the first permanent settler, had insisted that it be changed to Hood River.

Indian trails

Indians from the lower river had passed regularly along both banks of the Columbia before the uprisings of 1856-57 on their way to the great gathering places around The Dalles. There Northwest tribes met at the potlatches to barter, hunt fish and compete in games of physical skill.

Other Indians bound to and from the Willamette Valley used a trail said to have been cut by Hudson's Bay company trappers many years before. From The Dalles, this pass through the Cascades came over Seven-Mile Mountain to Mosier and across Hood River Valley.

Old valley trails

One trail came by the route of the present Old Mosier road, which is still negotiable. Other footpaths from The Dalles broke through farther south in to the valley. They converged at the ford of Neal's creek near Fike's corner, from where the main trail went west over Dethman ridge and … into Odell approximately 100 yards from the location of Wy'east high school. From there the going was level, following the present route of the Dee secondary highway to the ford of Hood river's west fork near Dee.

In the west hills the Indians could turn south along the present Lolo pass route and down Clear fork of the Sandy river. Or they continued westerly above Dee past Sandy Flat to Lost lake, Bull Run river and on to Milwaukie and Oregon City.

Rev. Daniel Lee, nephew of the famous emigrant leader Jason Lee, had brought the first herd of cattle into The Dalles area over this trail in the fall of 1838. He drove his charges from the Willamette mission over the hazardous Indian trail past Lost lake, Hood River Valley and Mosier. Lee Pack and Supply Trail (or the Lee Cattle Trail) was named in his honor.

Practically tropical

Shades of another mild winter come to light. Mrs. Ed Lage reminds us of records from the Nathaniel Coe family, first white

(continued)

people to live in Hood River after the terrible winter suffered from the Farnsworths and Laughlins in 1852. Coming in 1854, the Coes luckily had a balmy winter and noted that, in the early part of February 1855, they planted a half-acre in garden, one that produced bountifully.

Feb. 13, 1958

— ᴄᴙ —

Hood River County just 100 years ago, Part 2

Pioneer farming

By the spring of 1855 the Coes had brought cows, work oxen, horses, seeds and shrubs from Portland to their Hood River home. From the Luelling nursery at Milwaukie, first nursery in the state, and from Rochester, N.Y., they had obtained pears, peaches, cherries, plums, grapes, apricots, strawberries, gooseberries, currants and rose bushes.

Many apple seeds were planted on the Coe farm. Mrs. Coe had saved them from a bushel of apples she peeled while waiting at the lower Cascades for passage up the river to her new home. The Coes later in years sold nursery stock to other settlers and they were able to offer 38 known apple varieties, 31 unknown. By the winter of 1855-56 the Coes reported their roothouse and cellars were filled, the barn full of hay, grain, corn fodder and corn for the hogs.

In February 1856 the uprising of the Yakima and Klickitat Indians forced all white settlers here to flee to the army post at Fort Dalles, although the local Indians remained friendly, assisting the whites in some skirmishes along the river.

Indians in 1859

When the Coes came to Hood River in 1854 Henry, then a boy of nine, was of as much interest to the friendly Wasco Indians here as they were to him. A century ago he was welcome to roam the village called Waucoma, "place of the cottonwoods," which stood in the general vicinity of the [former] Safeway parking lot and railroad depot. The Wasco village, which had been seen by Lewis and Clark in 1859, consisted of 15 or 16 camps, as well as Henry Coe could later remember.

A half-dozen camps stood at Polalli-Illahee west of Hood River. A small group of Indians camped on a stream later to be known as Indian creek. Each camp consisted of from 10 to 15 adults. Although Coe found them "honest, truthful, generous and affectionate," he described them as fish-eating Indians who were "a squat ill favored, filthy crowd, reeking in dried salmon fumes and alive with vermin of various kinds."

First wagon

Because of the mountainous topography surrounding Hood River, no wagons arrived in the valley until 1862. In that year Davis Divers and his family drove a wagon and yoke of oxen from Oregon City to the Summit district west of Odell, to the astonishment of the few settlers in the valley at that time.

Divers had come east from Oregon City by way of the Barlow toll road to The Dalles. From there he brought the wagon, still on its own wheels, over the Lee Cattle Trail into the valley, the first rolling vehicle to arrive.

News of statehood

News of Oregon's admission to the Union did not reach Portland until March 15, 1859, [a month] after the actual vote and adoption by Congress on February 14 of that year. It is reasonable to assume, then, that the Coes, the Bensons, the Jenkins and the others in this isolated community did not receive the news until even later.

Whether these people favored statehood or not will never be known. But that they saw the promises of Hood River Valley clearly enough to endure hardship and loneliness is apparent from their honorable history.

First families

One hundred years ago today the Nathaniel Coe family had been living in Hood River over four years. In 1851 Mr. Coe, soldier, lawyer, merchant and amateur horticulturist, had been appointed United States postal agent for the Oregon territory including all land north of the California line and west of the Rockies. As agent, he let contracts for the Pony express, mail service, boat service, established new post offices and approved existing offices. In 1855 he retired from this position.

When he came to Hood River in June 1854 as leader of the first permanent white settlement here, Coe was 66 years of age. Of all the vast Oregon territory he had come to know, he chose Hood River Valley for his home.

The Coe Donation Land Claim filed in 1854 included land east of 13th street to the Hood river and north to the Columbia. Nathaniel Coe built his home above a spring, at approximately Sherman avenue between 10th and 11th streets. The spring was north of State street, between the present Wells and Huotte homes. Lumber for the house was rafted upriver from the Bradford mill on the Washington side of the Cascades. The Coe home consisted of one 20x40-foot room without ceilings or partitions.

The Coe family in 1859 included Mr. and Mrs. Coe, he then being 71 years of age, and sons Eugene, Charles and Henry. Another son, Lawrence, worked at the Cascades for the Bradford brothers. He later built and piloted steamboats on the Columbia for many years.

Coe neighbors

On February 14, 1859 William Jenkins and his wife were living in their substantial cabin west of the intersection of State and 13th streets, not far from the Coes. The Homestead had been built during the disastrous winter of 1851-52 by Dr. Farnsworth, who did not stay even a year.

James Benson and his bride Margaret were homesteading on Indian creek 100 years ago. Nathan and Martha Benson had built a cabin on their DLC east of the Hood river, on the site of the present Harry English home. Jenkins and Nathan Benson had come to Hood River with Mr. Coe in 1854.

First industry

Out in the present Frankton district, A.C. Phelps had located the year before on the creek now bearing his name. He had a purpose in settling on Phelps creek, where the oaks grew thick. The gold miners in eastern Oregon were clamoring for whiskey, which could only be packed into isolated areas in kegs slung over the backs of mules.

Phelps, a cooper [barrel-maker] by trade, manufactured and shipped five-gallon oak kegs to The Dalles by water as one of Hood River's first industries. S.B. Ives was his partner and it is assumed that both men were here on February 14, 1859.

Other settlers

Local historical records gathered by Mrs. T.R. Coon mention a Mr. Cowperthwaite who secured land adjoining the Phelps farm and who spent the winter of 1858 with Phelps.

Sometime early in 1859 John M. Marden filed a pre-emption claim on land along the river west of Mitchell's point. The site had formerly been occupied by a warlike tribe of Indians under Chief Walluchian. It was called Polalli-Illahee by the natives, meaning "sand land." To get to Hood River Marden followed an Indian trail as it wound 400 feet up the sharp bluff since known as Ruthton hill.

On the east side of the valley in February 1859 there were a few settlers: the A.C. Stadden family and Arthur and Henry Gordon. In early February a Mr. Butler selected a homesite near the Stadden cabin, but Mrs. Butler and the M.M. Whitings did not arrive until March. Butler later sold his holdings to William Odell. These people, then, comprised the entire white population of Hood River Valley in 1859, so far as can be found from old records.

Northbank settlers

Closest white people to the tiny settlement of Hood River were Mr. and Mrs. E.S. Joslyn, who had homesteaded on the site of Bingen, Wash., in 1853. Their buildings were burned by Indians in 1856, after they had fled to the Cascades. When they returned later, the government had built a blockhouse at White Salmon where Alfred Townsend, an Indian agent, was living.

The family of Rev. E.P. Roberts, a retired missionary to the South Pacific, had also settled nearby. The Joslyns brought the J.R. Warner family, formerly from Massachusetts, to homestead near them. Thus the communities of White Salmon and Bingen were occupied in 1859.

At the Cascades

In old records, George Attwell or Atwell was referred to as justice of the peace at the Cascades in 1854, when Wasco county was created. The Roger Attwell family had settled at the Cascades in 1853, alongside the claim of John Chipman, who was named constable at the Cascades in the same records of 1854.

Farther west, Col. Joseph S. Ruckel, builder of the Oregon Portage, had homesteaded on the south bank of the Columbia, between Cascade Locks and Eagle creek at the middle Cascades. He had been the first civilian to cross the Isthmus of Panama in 1845 and later was a merchant in San Francisco Yerba Buena before coming to Oregon.

Mosier beginnings

East of Hood River Jonah H. Mosier homesteaded on a creek early in the '50s. He erected a sawmill there in 1855 and founded the town named after him. The Mosiers were forced to leave during the Indian trouble, but returned and added new buildings to their farm, which had become a stopping place for trail travelers.

The mill, which had proved profitable for several years, was later washed away and rebuilt, the Mosier buildings burned still later, but Jonah Mosier continued to rebuild and prosper modestly from various enterprises.

Feb. 12, 1959

— ભ —

CITY PARK BOASTS NATIVE AMERICAN HISTORY

When picnickers and children enjoy the shade of the little city park at 13th and State, they are standing where many Indians once camped, where war councils were held and the peacepipe smoked.

Eph Winans in his remembrances said, "I remember Chief Joseph in Indian council here on the grounds where the Camp Fire Girls reserve park is situated. He would stand alongside General Howard with his hand on the general's shoulder, a display of friendship for the Indian's good friend."

July 13, 1961

— ભ —

ADDRESSES, SIMPLIFIED

It wasn't a pretty young thing attracting attention downtown at the tail end of 1966. It was an old number — a 1914 Hood River phone book rescued from an old house by Elmer Hood. We've been promised a peek at this precious old directory of the Oregon-Washington Telephone Company wherein addresses are given, as, for example, "J.W. Cooper ... next to last house on Cascade."

Jan. 5, 1967

— ભ —

THE NAME STARVATION

For the Portland couple who asked about Starvation Creek's history, a short repeat. The secluded waterfall and small gorge west of Viento were not themselves involved in the happening which gave them their name. They were, at the time, buried under ice and snow.

It was on the railroad tracks below, laid only two years before, that the great train drama of December 1884 and January 1885 began. Those who almost starved were 148 passengers and crew members.

> Dec. 10, 1884 — A winter storm began with snow and high winds which were to continue until after New Year's day.

> Dec. 16 — A westbound passenger train got as far as Hood River behind a plow and three engines, but backed to The Dalles again.

> Dec. 18 — Four trains waiting at The Dalles were combined behind two engines behind a snowplow to make a run for it through the Gorge. The track was clear to Hood River.

Two miles below Viento, probably somewhere east of Shell Rock mountain, the engines rounded a curve and ran into snow 20 to 25 feet deep which had slid down the slope.

Crew and men passengers shoveled, but another slide roared down, almost burying the engines. The trains consisted of 148 people in approximately 30 units. There was no backing up because snow now blocked the rear of the train.

Sack lunches only

Food was the immediate concern. There were no dining cars then. Most passengers had sack lunches with them to serve as supper before what had been expected to be a late evening arrival in Portland.

An inventory of the baggage car turned up three cases of oysters, two quarters of beef, one mutton and 50 to 75 jackrabbits. Fuel was also in short supply.

Other trains stopped

The ordeal lasted three weeks. All trains became stalled, by snow and by an accident which shoved several emergency engines off the track near Viento.

Food was brought by Hood River men on snowshoes, as long as the supplies here lasted. Food which was cooked when it left town was frozen when it reached the passengers.

Christmas and New Years rolled past. Measles broke out. On Jan. 2, the train was able to move forward to Bonneville. By Jan. 6 the warming Chinook wind opened the track so that the last barrier at Oneonta gorge could be broken through.

Early the next day, Jan. 7, at 2 a.m. the jinxed train rolled into the Portland station. What stories those 148 people must have had to tell!

May 21, 1970

— CR —

HISTORY THROUGH YOUNG EYES

[Fourth-grader Phillip Rotter's interview of Mace Baldwin last Tuesday in Hood River] became the sixteenth in a series of interviews for a project now receiving the serious attention of the Oregon Historical Society and a small operating fund from the federal government.

The interview with Mr. Baldwin followed a pattern developed by Mrs. Elma Rives since she started the local history project in 1970 for her 4th grade classes at Parkdale Elementary School.

Phillip introduced himself and identified Mr. Baldwin for the benefit of the taped record which was rolling. He then asked Mace some "leading" questions about his boyhood as the son of the earliest

(continued)

permanent homesteader in the Upper Valley, long before the town of Parkdale existed.

They were "leading" questions because Mrs. Rives and her co-worker, Myrna Higgins, had already talked to Mace in order to outline the main topics Phillip was to ask about. They had found that this pre-run cut down the time of the students' interview and zeroed in on important history facts.

This novel approach developed by Mrs. Rives benefits the youngsters by bringing them into personal contact with those who have lived local history. And it adds a permanent record of Hood River's story through the tape recordings and the additional material Mrs. Higgins takes into shorthand and types up from the initial interview she and Mrs. Rives attend.

The Oregon Historical Society saw so much value in Mrs. Rives' idea that Charles Achley, a staff member in charge of the "Man and the Land" federal project under the Joint Committee for the Humanities, arranged for $200 of its Oregon grant to go toward expenses of the local program — for tapes, photographs, travel and secretarial work.

The small grant was contingent upon sponsorships by the OHS and by the Hood River county school district. The local district has reproduced some of the tapes for its Audio-Visual Center. The state Historical Society is to copy the taped interviews and typewritten material for future use in its library.

Mrs. Rives took the first batch of tapes and manuscripts to the museum in Portland last Saturday. If the material passes muster, there is hope of more funds for continuing the gathering of local history.

How did the idea for the students' interviews with long-time Hood River people pop up?

"Out of frustration, I guess," Mrs. Rives admits. "There was so little 4th graders could read about local history — the Indians, the explorers and the pioneers."

Her search proved so futile that a do-it-yourself idea occurred to her. The tape-recorder, used in the classroom as a tool to help slower readers, touched it off. Why not tape the accounts of earlier days by those who lived them, she thought.

"This is a rich and fascinating area," she says now. "The interviews bring my children from a study of the general development of the Northwest down to one section — a microcosm, you might say — giving a picture of how the county developed. And, after all, Hood River is a prototype of all Oregon counties."

Do the 4th graders like to conduct the interviews? "They love them. They can't wait to do tapes!"

You get the feeling that Mrs. Rives' own love of history and her exhilaration over this new project gives it much of its momentum. Although she grew up in Texas, she has lived in Oregon and Idaho 30 years, has taught at Parkdale for 10 of them.

The class has guest speakers, too. Jack Cochran of Parkdale, who has made a study of "mountain men," was due to come this week, probably in his handmade buckskin suit and coonskin cap, with his handmade copy of an early rifle.

Jack has visited the class before. He showed the children the ancient art of soap carving.

Each of the interviews takes about six hours, counting the preliminary visit, outlining the questions and then the actual taped interview by the student. Not to mention the hours sorting material, arranging for visits and a dozen other details.

Some of the interviews have required three or even four visits by Mrs. Rives.

Why does she give so much of her own time and extra effort to the project?

"Because I love it!" the teacher admits.

But you know that her excitement over this vastly worthwhile work of gathering local historic data is not chiefly for her own pleasure.

(continued)

To a dedicated teacher like Elma Rives, the involvement of her youngsters is what really counts.

Not only do they get close to real history, the conversations, the study, the classroom visits are all woven into the children's daily school work: creative writing, spelling, even a bit of math and drama connected with the history search.

The sixteen tapings to date have been mostly with Parkdale people, but the area is being broadened.

Among those already interviewed are Martha Brunquist, Florence Euwer, Myrna Higgins and her mother, Mrs. Otis James; Ray Yasui, Mace Baldwin, Mr. and Mrs. Jess Hutson, Sydney Babson, Dave Cooper, Harold and Malcolm McIsaac, Alyuna Routson, Frances Doggett Rose, Elvira Kelly, Jack Cochran, and Mr. and Mrs. Mart Porterfield.

In the midst of a very busy time, Ray Yasui recently polished off the tape of his interview conducted by a nephew at four in the morning. Mrs. Rives finds such cooperation a spur to her project.

And so we salute the 4th grade classes at Parkdale with whom Elma Rives works. They are adding to the stock of historical data, both for Hood River and for Oregon.

To "teacher," our bronze medal with apple leaf clusters for her enormous but far from thankless project.

Mrs. Rives will welcome the names of other long-time local people who would contribute valuable data to the research.

Feb. 3, 1972

— ෴ —

CENSUS PROVES HISTORY BOON

Government statistics can be boring, but they often prove a boon to history.

An 1870 U.S. Census of Hood River and Falls Cascade Locks precincts, turned up in The Dalles library, gives the first good picture of present Hood River county as it was occupied at that time.

Taken 16 years after the first white families came here to stay, the census shows name, age, sex, state or country of origin, and occupation. It also indicates race, if other than white.

Hood River precinct, including the whole valley, lists 23 families totaling 85 people.

Among familiar names are Coe and Benson two of the four original Donation Land Claim settler-families, Neal, Turner, O'Dell, Divers, Stanley for whom Stanley rock at Koberg's beach is named, Tieman and Baldwin earliest homesteaders in the Upper Valley.

In the Falls precinct, now Cascade Locks, five families and 24 people are reported as of 1870. Of these, 12 are listed as "Indian" or as "breed," and some of these even more specifically as "1/2" or "1/4 breed." There is no listing for John Chipman, who had received the first DLC property given by the government in this area.

1972 Panorama, Hood River News

— ℃ℜ —

BLOSSOM DAY HISTORY

Here all this time it has been said that the official Blossom Day celebration in Hood River Valley is a fairly young tradition, going back only about 20 years.

Well, scrub that date! Change it to 1919, which was 54 years ago, when the very first Blossom Day Festival was held. And give credit not to local people but the Portland Advertising Club.

A certain Tad Hazen of Portland, a "real live wire" and probably related to Bob Hazen, had the idea as a "valid excuse to visit the valley."

(continued)

"Apple Blossom Day" they called it when it was planned in late April 1919.

This was no error. The apple was king of Hood River crops then — the Newtowns, Spitzenburgs and Ortleys, the Jonathans, Red Delicious and Winter Bananas.

Pears didn't amount to much in the valley in 1919. Out of total distribution of $500,000 to farmers for the 1918 crop handled by the young and growing Apple Growers Association, only $275,000 went for pears, cherries and strawberries all together.

The winter of 1919-20 was a holy terror. It killed thousands of young and established apple trees, many of which were replaced with pears by farmers who saw the handwriting on the wall.

But this was the winter after the first Apple Blossom Festival.

A smallish committee of local men was named by the Hood River Commercial Club in a half-hearted effort to humor the Portland fellows. There really wasn't much enthusiasm here for the Apple Blossom Day, which had been set for April 27.

Plans called for escorting the visitors to "Chautauqua Park" present site of Memorial hospital where they could eat lunch (hopefully, they would bring their own baskets!) with coffee provided, followed by "escorted tours" of the orchards in blossom.

"On leaving the park," reported the HR News, "every endeavor will be made to avoid raising the dust and therefore no fixed itinerary will be made, each driver following his own inclination."

A cold spell followed and the April 27 festival date was moved up to May 4.

However, a lot of Portland people had received word of the Festival but not of the postponement. Upward of 300 cars came from Portland to see the blossoms the next weekend.

Negotiation of the new, yet unpaved Columbia River highway was no small accomplishment in itself. It took close to three hours each way, climbing up and letting those 1918 touring cars down from Crown Point over the Latourell loops.

Hood River was not prepared for the sudden influx.

In a tone of awe and disbelief, the News reported that "one steady stream of cars arrived from Portland. Hotels and restaurants could not quite handle the wants of hungry visitors and every source of food supply was appealed to in the hope of being able to send all away satisfied."

It was chaotic!

Charlie and Ola Bell's Mount Hood hotel dining room overflowed. It was reported that good old Charlie had to go out to town in search of a sandwich that night.

The Oregon [present Hood River] hotel served over 300 on Sunday.

At her popular Cottage Farm Resort on Belmont road Alma Howe had to turn away 200 more than she could feed.

The story was the same at the Dickinson hotel, Hicks' restaurant, the Hood confectionary and the Chinese café.

The good people of Hood River were not blind. They got the message. By the following weekend, the new official date for the Festival, they were somewhat prepared.

People rolled into town on Saturday, May 3, and filled up overnight accommodations. Private residents were pressed into service for lodgings and meals. Carcasses of beef were hauled into all of the butcher shops.

By 9 a.m. Sunday morning, two troops of Boy Scouts were stationed at the top of Ruthton hill to direct visitors and to count them. In seven hours 717 cars and 37 motorcycles had arrived. The paper guessed that 5,000 people came.

Even a lady correspondent for the New York Herald Tribune appeared and had nice words for the valley and its blossoms.

A camp fire in the city park warmed the sightseers and the coffee. People who reclined on blankets feasted on the view and, presumably, on the basket lunches they had brought.

(continued)

There were Maypole dances in the orchards and guided tours and, we trust, not too much dust. It was a great weekend.

Another festival had been planned for 1920, but alas!

The killing winter of 1919-20 left a sad spring in its wake, with few blossoms and many dead trees.

Besides, the Columbia River highway was being paved at last and stretches of it were torture trails of sharp rock which ate up tires.

The HR Commercial Club and the Portland Advertising Club agreed to cancel Blossom weekend.

But that first year of the Festival had been a dinger!

WHERE DID THEY GO FOR FUN?

Where did Hood River people go for entertainment in the good ol' days? Why, to the train depot, of course!

"Down at the station" was the town's glamour spot from the time the steam engines first came in 1882 until the Columbia River highway in 1920 offered an alternative way to travel in and out of Hood River.

Socially and business-wise, it was smart to be seen at the station, greeting prominent visitors and newcomers, being seen as you arrived or departed on the train.

On the other hand, if you had mischief on your mind it was no good trying to sneak out of town. The editor of the local weekly paper spotted all arrivals and departures and duly reported them.

The only other way to go was by steamer and the editor always seemed to be at the boat landing, too.

In early days business men took their sack lunches down by the tracks if there was a train around noon. "Going to the station" provided a Sunday afternoon's entertainment, or a nice evening's stroll.

Everyone knew the train schedule. By 1910 four passenger trains came through Hood River daily, two of them transcontinental. First class fare to Chicago was $67.65. Tourist class was $12 less. It was a trip of three days and three nights.

Arriving here, a stranger to the town found a convenient flight of long, white stairs leading directly from the depot to Cascade avenue and then on up to the big, hospitable verandah of the rambling old Mount Hood hotel which loomed above the railroad tracks.

People claimed that the biggest deals in the valley's boom times were made at that hotel, in the lobby, on the big porch or in the spacious dining room.

Real estate agents worked out of their hats from the hotel. They would glad-hand likely looking prospects at the coach steps, then lead them up the stairs to their lairs in the Mount Hood lobby.

If the newcomer sparked to the agent's glowing description of the valley, he was whisked out for a brief — very brief — look at acreages. The deal was often sewed up over dinner in the hotel dining room.

The pace was slower at the train station in an earlier day, before the orchard boom. Station agent E.C. Mooney was reported by the local paper to spend his spare time shooting flies off boxcars on the siding with a peashooter he had made.

A new fashion brought men to watch the trains with more than average interest in the early 1900s. It was the day of the hobble skirt, the first breakaway from ankle-length skirts.

With luck, when a woman passenger came down those high steps from the coaches, the cluster of male onlookers might glimpse the calf of a pretty leg.

April 12, 1973

— ℭℜ —

THE COTTAGE FARM RESORT

[The following column was written after announcement that the original core building of the Hood River Care Center would be razed.]

First you have to get the picture of Hood River settlement in 1864.

When the original settlers came 10 years before, in 1854, three of their four Donation Land Claims took up all of the land along the Columbia river. When others came to the remote, isolated valley after the Indian troubles of 1856, the available farm land on the lower west side had to be outside the perimeter of the large Coe, Jenkins and James Benson Donation Land Claims.

The Coes' 320 acres covered what is today the major part of Hood River city to 13th street. The Jenkins' 320 acres reached from the Columbia west of today's 13th street south to present Belmont. Benson located on Indian creek.

By 1864 small farms were being hewed out of the forests beyond these DLC boundaries. There were also a few in the Pine Grove and Odell areas. And there existed a need for a school on the west side. By that time less than 80 people lived in the valley, but most of them were in this location.

The one-room school was built by the settlers about 1864 at the southwest corner of William Jenkins' DLC, which he gave for that purpose. The site today is a few hundred yards west of the Hood River Care Center on the Chuck Campbell property.

Lumber for the 14x20-foot schoolhouse came from the mill at the Cascades. With a 10x16 addition several years later, the building served until a school was built at Barrett in 1879 and another at Frankton in 1880.

The abandoned schoolhouse on Belmont, then known as Lyman Smith avenue, was purchased for 20 bushels of wheat, moved down the road and made into a comfortable pioneer home.

In 1885 Mrs. Alma Howe bought 40 acres at the present site of the Hood River Care Center and lived in the former schoolhouse on her property.

When she started her Cottage Farm Summer Resort in 1894, it soon became a popular retreat for wealthy summer guests and she built the present large structure around the small 1864 schoolhouse. It served as kitchen and family dining room during her long operation of the resort.

So that is why, when the old core building goes down this spring so, too, will Hood River's first schoolhouse.

Feb. 23, 1978

—∞—

ICE AGE

Ice was an early industry in Hood River. In February 1887 the Portland Natural Ice Co. put up a warehouse along the Columbia here. It would hold 20,000 tons.

Ice was then 14 inches thick. Blocks 22 inches square were cut from the "long slough" near present Wells island, were tossed on an endless chain and conveyed to storage, to be shipped to Portland and San Francisco. Cost to the company was 13 cents a ton.

The business prospered until 1900, but then a number of winters passed without ice in the river. Meantime, artificial ice-making had been invented. And anyhow, the local ice plant burned down in July 1900.

Feb. 14, 1980

—∞—

A "DRY" TOWN

Hood River was one of the driest settlements in the west until this century. When the town was platted by the Coes in 1881, and long afterward, you couldn't buy a business lot without promising never to make or sell liquor on the property.

(continued)

Way back in the 1860s, Arthur Phelps had a mill on the creek named for him where he made oak kegs, Hood River's first industry. They were sent — empty — by steamer to The Dalles and used to transport liquor to men working mines in eastern Oregon and Idaho. There certainly were no spirits distilled here in commercial quantities.

March 13, 1980

— CR —

Mount St. Helens blew its stack in 1842

[This column was written after the 1980 eruption of Mount St. Helens.]

Only two mentions of Mount St. Helens in its 19th century eruptions have been found in Hood River historical data so far.

When the action began on the snowcap in November 1842, Chinookian Indians occupied their Waucoma camp, "place of the cottonwoods," in an area directly above the railroad station. Henry Coe estimated that there were 150 natives here when his family came 12 years later. The only white people in the valley when St. Helens acted up would have been trappers and hunters for the Hudson's Bay Company.

In later years One-Eyed Susan, a very ancient native who had come to Hood River early in the century, said she remembered when St. Helens blew much of its top.

The only other report was from a Mrs. Garrison of the Barrett district. Henry Coe wrote that "she was the only white person I ever met who remembered the eruption of Mount St. Helens in 1846, when the east side of the crater was blown out." The Garrisons came to Oregon off the Oregon Trail that year.

April 10, 1980

— CR —

Mount St. Helens spoke its mind

"The ejected ashes were falling with a mist-like appearance, covering the leaves, fences and stones with a light, fine gritty substance, in appearance like hoar frost."

Written recently [during current Mount St. Helens eruption]? No, on Nov. 30, 1942, by Daniel Lee, founder of the Methodist Episcopal mission in The Dalles, following an eruption of Mount St. Helens.

Rip-roarin' Saturday nights

Memories of the 1920s and 1930s also recall Saturday nights in Hood River when stores on Oak Street stayed open until 9 p.m. and everyone in the county came to town.

Saturday night was a social event — the end of a hard week's work for all, including the children whose reward was a nickel for an ice cream cone. The Rialto might be showing Garbo and Gilbert in "The Flesh and the Devil," pretty racy stuff for Hood River. The KP band played lustily if not always in harmony from a portable stand at Second and Oak.

July 31, 1980

— ❧ —

The light side of Hood River history

So here I am, back to Hood River history again — the light side. Some of you are new here and I hope that you who have heard it before have short memories.

Native personalities

About our native people — the last two in Hood River, Charley and Alice Slimjim, are remembered by long-time residents and by boys who were young then. I'm sure our son, Christopher, then

(continued)

—27—

5 or 6, remembers Charley loved to ride his horse in any local parade in full native dress, his mocassined feet tucked up behind the saddle horn. On his usually immobile face would be a mischievous grin that said, "Look, kids! No feet!"

In the early 1950s, then an old man, he met Mrs. Norvin Coulter in the bank. She had been head of the local ration board during the war and Charley knew her well. She was at least 50 years younger than he. In a very loud voice full of surprise he said to her, "You still alive?"

After my father retired from his furniture store, now Van Metre's, he repaired sewing machines to keep busy. He was astonished that, as he was leaving the little shop, Charley would open the door and stand back for Alice; in his 35 years in Hood River, he had never seen such courtesy shown an Indian woman who, on the sidewalk, always walked behind her man.

Alice spent her last days at Hanby's Nursing Home. A local woman used to visit her regularly to wash and plait her waist-long black hair.

There were natives living in Hood River into this century. One lady who arrived in 1911 from the East always remembered an incident at the railroad depot. Near the station stood a group of young Indian men and, a little way off among the cottonwoods on the banks of the Columbia, a circle of Indian women. When the women's tight circle stirred, a new baby's cry was heard, and the men began clapping a young Indian man on the back. A new father! This must have happened during the strawberry season when the Indians were here to pick.

Over the years, stories were told of George Tomileck Chinidere, who had long lived in a tiny house along the Columbia. He died under a freight train when he was on his way home in 1917. George was Catholic, but in the winter he chose Asbury Methodist, where he had his pew by the warm furnace. He was famous for his amazingly accurate predictions of severe winters. When asked how he could tell that a hard winter was coming, George answered frankly, "White man put in plenty wood!"

George once came into the huge sum of $1500. He was a Yakima Indian. A local lawyer, John Leland Henderson, advised him to open a checking account at a local bank. Henderson did not like the bank owners. He wrote out checks and showed George how to make his mark when he cashed them. George gleefully spread checks downtown, all of them for five cents or no more than 10 cents. The banks were furious; one month George cashed over 20 checks.

Alma Howe, who opened her Cottage Farm summer resort in 1894 on the present site of the HR Care Center and ran it until 1931, was guardian angel to all local Indians. One autumn Charley asked her if she would keep his three ponies for the winter. She told him that she hadn't time to do so, and he replied, "That's all right. George come live with you and take care of them."

Conspicuous consumption

When the only road to The Dalles went up out of Pine Grove, a family lived at the top of Hood River Mountain. On the road in front of their house was a huge chuckhole. When there was lots of rain, the husband charged $5 to pull those new-fangled cars out of the mud. And it was rumored that, when no rain occurred, he kept the hole filled with water anyway.

The Hood River period of Conspicuous Consumption was full of stories. When hard-working, pioneer orchardists and strawberry growers had made Hood River's name famous around the country for its scenery and its fruit, a wealthy, slightly madcap group arrived to "play," and what color they added to the little community!

"Cap" McCan

Capt. Charles McCan arrived in 1910 at age 24. He had a steamboat captain's license, since one of his grandfathers owned a steamer line in the south. "Cap" was heir to New Orleans fortunes from both sides of his family and it was told to me by a man who knew him well that he arrived with a suitcase containing $100,000 in cash which he dumped down in front of

(continued)

an astonished teller at the local bank. He brought his current love, Carmen, and he had come because young men he had known in school in Switzerland who were then living here had urged him to come.

Cap had his southern-style house built on Tucker road where it still stands with its Italian marble fireplace and chandelier by Tiffany, but the special kitchen for his chef has been altered. There was a big barn for his thoroughbred horses and a racetrack.

He stayed three years the first time, importing the first Lozier sedan on the Pacific coast, called a "tonneau" because the seating compartment was separate from the chauffeur's section. A local lady says that, when high school classes heard the Lozier coming, everyone went to the windows to watch it pass by. Often, she said, Cap would be driving, his chauffer riding on a special seat built on the running board.

Dr. Adams

Dr. William Adams was the third doctor of sorts in the valley. After a varied career, he got his medical degree in one year at the age of 56. He owned — rather, his wife bought — the Donation Land Claim of 320 acres which is now 13th street from the Columbia river up to May street and west. Mrs. Adams divorced him in 1878, a year after coming to HR.

He built a sanitarium just below where today Sherman avenue swings west off 13th street. It was to care for men working on the first railroad through the Columbia Gorge. He also treated local patients and was later said to have overcharged them mightily. One of his hobbies was writing vitriolic letters to the Hood River Glacier criticizing everything in town and valley.

On his "Paradise Farm," as he called it, he had a pet sturgeon in a pool on the landscaped grounds. The sturgeon grew and grew. Doc died in 1906 and soon afterward his second wife, who had been Sue Mosier of Mosier, had the huge fish taken to the Columbia. It had outgrown the shallow pool and became terribly sunburned. It headed for the depths without a goodbye.

The tombstone Dr. Adams designed for himself in Idyllwild cemetery was, like him, an enigma. A folklorist at the U of O who examined it in the 1970s called it "Adams' conceit."

Above a conventional, square granite shaft with a gothic pyramid top, one would expect to find a conventional cross. Not Dr. A., who had quarreled with Christianity, as well as with everything else. Instead of a cross on top, a solid granite block was balanced precariously on one of its own corners. The U of O man had also discovered that the cube on top lined up exactly with the west slope of Mount Adams and with the west slope of Mount Hood. The monument, standing seven feet high, had the name "Adams" twice and a capital "A" five times.

Some time in the 1970s the cube was stolen and never found. It weighed at least 100 pounds.

Gentlemen farmers and enterprising folks

There were local jokes in the early 1900s about the young men coming to start orchards here with no knowledge of farming. One amateur plowed an acre on his ranch and bought a bushel of corn-on-the-cob from a neighbor. Later he came to plant three more bushels. Come to find out, he had been advised by locals to plant a whole ear of corn in each hole.

One Easterner was told that he should shake bees up every morning before putting them out to pollanize the fruit blossoms. A hired hand loaded the hives on a wagon and hauled them around and around the orchard. Not surprisingly, every bee smothered to death.

Trafford Smith, a bonvivant from the East whose wealthy mother had staked him to a good, producing orchard on Tucker road in the early days, had a wonderful crop of apples one autumn, so he hired men to knock the fruit off the trees. That way, he could write Mama that he had no crop and would she please send more money!

(continued)

In the 1890s Ned Marshall's grandfather, Sam Bartmess, sold Victor bicycles along with his furniture and mortuary business. Bicycling was very "in" then, before cars.

At that time the Heights from 12th street east to the Hood river was a park-like wilderness. Sam, with a good eye for business, hired six or eight men and a team to clear and smooth a cycle path, all in one afternoon. He called it Cycle avenue, a circle of sorts, 1-1/2 miles around and almost level. There were even two-bike stalls so that one could leave his vehicle there. No parking rules or red tape then. No zoning rules.

There were no arrests for speeding, no fatalities and only one collision. A gentleman rider, waiting 20 feet off the path, was hit by a lady cycler. But there was no injury and no lawsuit.

May 1989 speech to the local Philanthropic Educational Organization (PEO)

— ❧ —

HOSPITAL ON CHAUTAUQUA GROUNDS

The new hospital stands on ground that has great memories for old-timers. In 1914, the Chautauqua open-air amphitheater stood there among big trees. It was a purely local production of Gilbert and Sullivan's "The Mikado," deemed a huge success. Attorney-basso George Wilbur sang the title role, a parade featured local Japanese boys in costume, and Japanese gentlemen comprised the chorus.

In later years, the official Chautauqua Institute sent a summer week's worth of lecturers, political figures, comics, musicians and other "cultural" programs. High entertainment for little Hood River, and especially enjoyable for mosquitoes, with at least 100 present to enjoy every ticket holder.

Dec. 12, 1990

— ❧ —

HUMOR PREVAILED IN PIONEER TIMES

Hood River and its valley may appear laid back and creaky to high-energy newcomers, but its history is sprinkled with smiles, unique and vigorous people and hints of how tough pioneer life was.

In earlier times, Hood River had winters that today's residents cannot imagine. One old-timer swore how, in 1919-20, when about half of the fruit trees in the valley were killed, milk froze between the cow and the bucket.

Pauline Keller Windell remembers that, in deep snow, Franz's dairy delivered milk from a big sled. "The milk would freeze and punch the stopper up, and we would bite off the cream on top."

When Hood River winters were worst, the Columbia River often froze solid and a herd of cattle could be driven across it. In 1910, Otis Treiber operated a ferry from Underwood, Wash., to the Oregon side. He boasted that his little boat never stopped. "As long as there was a two-bit fare I always found a way to break through the ice, go around or drive over it."

From a Hood River Public School Regulation in 1902: "Any pupil who shall show disrespect toward teachers or other persons, whether on or off the school grounds, shall be liable for suspension or other punishment." Which no doubt meant the corporal kind.

Pioneer Capt. Henry Coe built his second Hood River boat in 1892, the little propeller-driven Irma. He said she could go anywhere. When the Columbia River rose to its highest in recorded history, he proved it.

The June 23, 1894 The Dalles Chronicle reported: "Captain H.C. Coe came up from Hood River yesterday morning on his little steamer Irma, making the run in three hours. The trip was made part of the way overland, the little boat coming over the meadows and fields and part of the way taking straight cuts through the cottonwoods.

"On one of those cut-offs, the boat ran aground under full speed and the captain and crew, engineer and passengers had to remove their trouserloons and climb out to push it off."

(continued)

A quick way to lose weight: In August 1898, local attorney John Leland Henderson swam from Hood River to Cascade Locks, accompanied by Ephram Winans in his small boat. He swam the 20 miles without losing a single stroke and he lost five pounds.

In November of the same year he biked to The Dalles on railroad tracks, there being no road along the Columbia. Coming home, he met a train on one of the highest trestles near Mosier, but dismounted safely. It was not reported whether he lost weight on that trip.

In early days a couple named Arnold lived in the Lower Valley close to the west hills. One day Mr. Arnold came home empty handed from a hunting trip but Mrs. Arnold showed him her own trophy, a large and handsome but very dead cougar. The cat had been after her chickens until she cornered it and shot it under her house.

A pioneer farm family living on the present site of Hood River Valley High School could, in their day, only get to town by opening and then closing behind themselves and their horses, 17 gates along Brookside Drive.

Homer Van Allen operated the last Hood River ferry across the Columbia before the interstate bridge was built in 1924. His dock and his home were on the present site of the Inn at Hood River Village.

First in line each morning for passage to the Washington side was his own little Jersey cow, who loved the lush pastures around Bingen. But she was always first in line to come home on the last trip of the day.

April 27, 1991

— CR —

CHAPTER 2

GORGE TREASURES

— Snippets of area interest

SIGNS-OF-THE-SEASON DEPT.

The bobtailed junco feeding in the yard probably suffered this indignity at the paws of pussy. The loss hasn't impaired his appetite one bit, although his flight is a little erratic … Straws in the local political wind? Two friends are planning to change their registration so they can vote for Ike … Don't forget to signal with your porch light Thursday night between 7 and 8 p.m. that you have a March of Dimes contribution for the mothers who will be out collecting in the cold, cold night.

June 28, 1952, Hood River Daily Sun

— ೞ —

WHERE'S OREGON?

Aside from all the politicking, Senators Morse and Neuberger are accomplishing one Herculean and historic task for which we should ever be grateful. They are making the country aware that a state named Oregon does, in fact, exist!

Most anyone traveling east of the Mississippi has been painfully reminded that, in the minds of many Americans, Oregon simply doesn't exist, or at best, is a forgotten packet of land "somewhere off up there," with a vague wave toward Alaska. Travel articles, with few exceptions, leave the impression that Los Angeles occupies the southern half of the Pacific coast and California the rest.

Returning one time from the east, we were plunged into despair by the conviction that those back-easters who have heard of Oregon seriously think we live in teepees and spend Saturday nights dodging bullets behind the swinging doors of the Last Chance saloon.

One Oregon couple, traveling in New England, came upon a storekeeper who confessed she had never heard of Oregon. What a shock to our regional ego!

(continued)

So, by repetition, that great and gnawing technique so artfully employed to imprint ideas in the public cranium, the headlines for Senators Sr. and Jr. may wake the nation to the fact that Oregon has joined the Union.

WESTERN NAMES

Flavor of the old west does linger in many of our geographic names around Oregon. Douglas County has its Dread and Terror Ridge, so named because of the dense thickets which made fire-fighting difficult.

Over in Harney County there's a little stream with a big handle — Donner and Blitzen River. No dear, not named for Santa's transportation! It was christened during the Snake War of 1864 when troops crossing it during a thunder storm gave it the German name for thunder and lightning.

Feb. 11, 1955

— ❧ —

SPRING WITH A CAPITAL "S"

Spring, even if it be a false one, was spelling its name with a capital "S" in the valley earlier this week. All the signs were there: The b-r-r-r of tractors and spray rigs ... orchard implements being oiled and greased and gassed ... pruned limbs thick under the trees ... tennis games at the high school ... "cats" trodding heavily as they pulled out old orchards for new ventures ... bees bustling around the jasmine ... bonfires with weenie roasts in the evening ... small boys cooking supper over pit fires ... folks tentatively removing an outer layer of coats and sweaters.

Feb. 18, 1955

— ❧ —

News of high places

Next to Mount Hood, our own Mount Defiance on the west side of Hood River Valley is the highest peak in the entire region of the Columbia Gorge on the Oregon side. It is 4,960 feet.

Wonder if the large granite boulder is still atop Van Horn Butte in Pine Grove? Geologists think it could have been stranded there by floating ice.

Van Horn Butte itself is a cinder crater from a comparatively recent eruption. Booth Hill above Odell, on the other hand, is an old protruding basalt hill.

Clay banks along the Mount Hood Railroad switch-back south of Powerdale and at other points along the Hood River prove, by their scattered pebbles and boulders, that they are glacial "till" laid down by moving melting ice. Hood River itself is still actively deepening every part of its gorge, a sign of youthfulness.

March 11, 1955

—CR—

Noble Mount St. Helens

Mount St. Helens, majestic as seen from Troutdale in the clear air these days, was first spotted by Lewis and Clark from the lower Columbia, near the present site of Longview. Lewis wrote in his diary: "It is the most noble looking object of its kind in nature."

April 8, 1955

—CR—

Cool picnic

That first optimistic picnic last week was a dilly! Never ate faster, never tasted better coffee, never found home toastier. And no birds. They were probably huddled together back in the woods, also swigging black coffee!

June 10, 1955

Lighten up, Oregon!

Oregon has one bad fault — that of taking itself too seriously. Admittedly, it's hard to smile on a dark day, but look what Texas and California have done with their more repulsive features … Turned them into national publicity and tourist money by laughing at themselves.

When Texas has a tornado, it's the BIGGEST. When Texas has a drought, it's the DRIEST. When L.A. has smog, folks come from all over just to appear in it!

Why doesn't Oregon make capital of its cool weather, smile through its chilblains? Why doesn't the Rose Festival parade show Paul Bunyan chopping down giant trees under a monstrous umbrella?

By golly, most of us wouldn't trade Oregon for anywhere else, so why don't we let the world know we've got the greenest green and the sunniest sun when it does peek through, instead of making our weather a "cause apologi" to the whole country. Remember — laugh and the world laughs with you; build a better mousetrap and the mice will weep!

June 17, 1955

— ❦ —

Anyone for a swim?

First-of-July scene: Lifeguard Alison Holdrige patrolling the swimming pool in rainslicker and hat, guarding one lone youngster in the water!

July 8, 1955

— ❦ —

How do you like them apples?

This is THE time of year! Green apple pie … apple dumplings … apple pandowdy … French apple cream pie from a good recipe by Mrs. Leroy Brant of Parkdale … apple tapioca … baked apples … Southern fried apples … but mostly applesauce on toast. We got the idea from Booth Tarkington's "Seventeen"— remember? — and it is the most!

Sept. 16, 1955

— ℞ —

No Love Here

There is nothing, absolutely nothing, so unloved as a harvest rain in Hood River Valley!

Oct. 14, 1955

— ℞ —

Tune That Bridge!

One of our smartest high school students, musically inclined, wishes to place a complaint with the HR port commission. The deck plates in the Interstate bridge, sez she, are not perfectly attune. The tonal difference between left and right tires falls short of being a full octave, and is thus annoying to sensitive ears. How about a new deck in perfect pitch?

Which reminds us that the littlest member of the family long ago christened it the "singing bridge" … only you can't get above middle "e" at the 25-mile speed limit!

Oct. 28, 1955

— ℞ —

Mount Rainier View

It's-news-to-me department: Always thought you had to be on a high, high hilltop to see Mount Rainier from this vicinity. But one of the best views of the snowcapped giant is from a stretch of

(continued)

the Loop highway just north of Cooper Spur junction. On a good day it also peeks through at a point on the Columbia water level highway about one-half mile west of the old Wyeth CCC camp.

Jan. 19, 1956

— ♋ —

SEASONAL SCENTS

Add to favorite winter smells… the tantalizing waft of split peas and ham bone simmered with a pinch of the herb called savory… The indefinable odor of that bear or goose grease applied to boots… The fragrance of falling snow. Indeed. It does have a smell all its own!

Jan. 17, 1957

— ♋ —

THINGS WERE DIFFERENT BACK THEN

No one denies young couples their modern, complete comforts, but we wonder what they'll have on which to look back and laugh at the memory. The generations who raised their families the hard way when Hood River was a pup, or during the depressions, have their laughingest moments over those tribulations.

Like backing the car up those steep grades to Cloud Cap Inn … the all-day trip to town from the Upper Valley … the army cot that served as a sofa … the cold, cold outhouse … those tenting trips to the beach when it took a long day to get there … the walking trips from Hood River to Portland which were the goal of every adventurous HR boy … taking a hack over the old, old road to Mosier, or up the east side grade … keeping baby chicks in the kitchen during those early, cold spring days … Saturday night in town, when a five-cent ice cream cone was the weekly treat for the whole family.

April 19, 1956

— ♋ —

Hey, Jupe Pluvius!

We love the sunshine and its warmth,
The bright increase in autumn tones,
But true Webfeet all wish for rain —
We need some moisture in our bones!

Sept. 26, 1957

— ❧ —

No place like home

Little valley of big vistas. Where the hand-hewn orchards roll away from the hills on three sides. Where the 11,245-foot marshmallow-topped sundae looks lickin' good on a sunshiny day. Where a red sun in the west dribbles it with strawberry syrup.

Hood River!

Where all the land runs downhill to the power-packed Columbia. Where all the barges and tugs and yachts and cabin cruisers rolled into one and simultaneously tooting their horns couldn't equal the thrill that folks felt when the S.S. Bailey Gatzert blew her mighty whistle on the old river run as she skirted the sandbars and cottonwoods coming in to dock.

Where old-timers mourn the passing of such river sports as sliding down the sand dunes … playing with the sluggish jack salmon caught by lower water on the bars … the everyday occurrence of arrowheads found anywhere around the mouth of the Hood river … swimming in the "long" slough and skating on the "round" slough, both of which claimed too many lives … walking the sandbars from Ruthton to the Hood river.

April 7, 1960

— ❧ —

Courtesy Trumps Fine

Evidence to support many Hood River merchants' belief that a courteous notice of an overparking violation on out-of-state tourists and even Oregon travelers' cars would do this city more good than the fifty-cent fine:

Earlier in September, Mr. and Mrs. T.D. Rasmussen arrived downtown from Mitchell, Neb. In their rush to greet their hosts, Mr. and Mrs. Blair Carpenter, they forgot the parking pennies. Instead of a red ticket when they returned, they found a polite reminder of the violation and a pictorial plug for Hood River Valley.

Mrs. Rasmussen later wrote the Carpenters that she'd like them to personally thank Ken Murphy, the officer who issued the courteous notice, for her. She added that she was keeping it as a souvenir of a most pleasant stay in Hood River where, incidentally, she had done a sizable amount of shopping.

Sept. 29, 1960

— ∞ —

Joys of Small-Town Living

You can have the city.

We'll take Hood River, where Blair Carpenter guesses about how much a very young lady can afford for a gift … Eleanor Lance remembers your friend's size … Marvin Harder has your husband's measurements … Jo Dethman takes time for a friendly word … Mark Clark knows what cosmetics mamas like … Gil Jubitz understands what tool you are trying to describe … Stella Bransky lets you shop in peace because she knows you are a slow decider … the Belluses will get it for you if they don't have it … a smile, a good laugh is included with every visit to Tucker's … you meet a host of long-time friends at McIsaac's … Mary Phillips runs out after you with the glove you left on Hickey's counter … Jerry Kramer knows how much air you carry in your tires.

Sophisticated shopping centers? We'll take Hood River and all its good people any time of the year.

Dec. 21, 1961

— CR —

ANOTHER VIEW OF THE VIEW

On Panorama Point Sunday, man looks impatiently at the view … where sun and clouds argue above the valley … where shafts of light pierce through to touch a block of white pear blossoms … where Mount Hood struggles to push out from under its cloud covering … where tidy green orchards stretch muscular rows for a glimpse of the sun.

And this man says to his wife, as he dives back into his car, "Ah, come on! There's nothin' to see here."

April 25, 1963

— CR —

WHENCE THE CONSTRUCTION?

Once the four-class HRHS reunion group had become Hood River oriented on July 25, the big question was: "Where is the money coming from for all these new homes? Hood River looks so prosperous, yet you haven't any industry to speak of!"

The old town did look good under the hot summer sun … with some old eye-sores in the main business districts cleared away … with homes and farms well-kept … with the waterfront and the S.S. Banning neat and shipshape … with the new highway approaches giving the town a busy, part-of-the-world look, compared with its once-isolated quietness.

Aug. 6, 1964

— CR —

All but Starvation

[after the Columbus Day Storm]

Even a bluejay wouldn't recognize them! All of the little state parks in Hood River county's end of the Gorge are in indescribable shambles, except Starvation creek.

Where Perham creek only last summer ambled gracefully down one side of Wygant park to the tune of hissing hamburgers, now a gray cascade of water falls flatly over a solid field of boulders, and over the old highway.

On to Viento, where generations have cooled their feet in the creek and scuffed through the forest duff under the big trees. Now it is a gray trench full of grimy water, and not a spot near the stream to set out a potato salad.

Worst shock of all

Lindsey creek is the worst shock of all, a scene of complete destruction from one wall of the little glen to the other. The glass, the tables, the stoves, even the restrooms are buried under four to six feet of basaltic and volcanic boulders.

Feb. 25, 1966

— ❧ —

Evens don't get fair share

"It's hardly fair," said Aunt Illi, scowling at the neighbor's sprinkler as it spouted water. "The odd numbers can sprinkle two days in a row every time there's a thirty-first of the month. That's May, July, August and October. Us evens never get such a break. Next time, I'm moving to an odd-numbered house!"

Aug. 4, 1966

— ❧ —

Traveler's reflection

One of the young people back from an American Heritage tour said that, after leaving the train at Bingen on the return trip, the view of Hood River from the interstate bridge was the most beautiful sight in America.

July 7, 1966

— ❧ —

Highway logic

The logic of highway pavement signs printed from bottom to top as you approach them escapes us. Few drivers can momentarily shift a lifetime habit of reading from top to bottom. So approaching the toll station at The Dalles bridge, you read

BACK
HURRY

In the city, the average driver reads from top to bottom, naturally

CROSSING
PEDESTRIAN

Jan. 26, 1967

— ❧ —

Famous Mitchell

Mitchell Point, the two-story basalt buttress four miles west of Hood River on U.S. 80N, has been many things to many people.

It was a landmark for early vessels on the Columbia river. A trial to early wagons and automobiles. An open-faced story of the Gorge to geologists.

The last, almost insurmountable Columbia River highway barrier was overcome by construction of the most unique tunnel in the United States.

(continued)

The two great abutments comprising the Point are Little Mitchell, rearing above the present highway, and Big Mitchell, rising 1,939 feet behind. Laid bare here is Columbia River basalt of the Miocene period, 12 to 28 million years old.

At the top of Big Mitchell geologists have identified a 100-foot thickness of quartzitic gravels cemented into columns and pinnacles. These deposits are overlain with Cascade lavas from the last period of vulcanism in the area.

Geologists believe the river gravels high atop Big Mitchell, similar to beds found at 100-foot elevation at the mouth of the Hood river, were carried to 2000-foot heights from the ancient Columbia river bed during the uplifting and folding of the Cascade mountains.

Naming of the Point is surrounded by pure legend. Some stories have a Captain Mitchell jumping his horse into the Columbia river rather than surrender to pursuing Indians during the Cascades Massacre of 1856.

Old timers denied the tale. Said Henry Coe, who had lived in Hood River two years when the Captain was supposed to have jumped, "There's not a shadow of truth in it. Mitchell Point was named after a man who took up a claim east of there."

One of the earliest steamboats, a converted schooner called the Mary, sank off Mitchell Point in 1857. She was miraculously salvaged, to run the river again.

Cattle herds moving downriver could skirt Mitchell Point on the river side. Before the Columbia River highway was built, buggies and a few cars could follow the old road which went up and over the saddle between Big and Little Mitchell. The grade was such that an auto going uphill had to be followed by someone carrying a large boulder to be shoved against a back wheel to prevent the car's running backward when the motor stalled.

Samuel Lancaster, builder of the original Columbia River highway, saw only one solution to Mitchell Point — to go through it. This he did in 1915, boring 400 feet through solid basaltic rock. The work, done mostly by hand, included hauling out the loose rock in wheelbarrows. Total cost of the tunnel was $50,000.

Actual engineering was done by J.A. Elliott, who fixed locations and directed construction for the work 100 feet above the railroad tracks. Lancaster got his idea for the great hole from the Axenstrasse tunnel in Switzerland, which had only three windows.

Mitchell Point tunnel boasted five great openings looking out over the Columbia.

When the water level highway was built around the base of Little Mitchell, the old tunnel was filled and sealed. In 1966 more of the base was blasted back to make room for the four-lane freeway.

April 28, 1967 Vacationer, Hood River News

— ❧ —

NAMES PROVIDE A KEY

A glossary of geographic names for Hood River Valley and neighboring points of interest pretty well defines the character of the people who first applied them. For the most part, they are no-nonsense names.

The early settlers were practical people. They had neither time nor inclination to think up romantic or catchy labels.

Names of pioneers came most easily. Memorializing them in the valley are the districts of Dee, Odell, Barrett, Frankton and Dukes Valley. The town of Mosier, six miles east, bears the name of its founder.

Neal, Baldwin and Phelps creeks in the valley, and many of the small streams running into the Columbia river, carry the names of early settlers. As do Cooper Spur, Eliot, Coe and Newton Clark glaciers on Mount Hood.

(continued)

A family name

Koberg's Beach on the Columbia is named for the family which developed it. Van Horn Butte, the knoll which rises abruptly on the lower east side of the valley, likewise.

Tucker road leads to Tucker bridge over the Hood river, where R.R. Tucker built a sawmill about 1883. Underwood mountain across the Columbia was settled by brothers Amos and Ed Underwood, who came in the 1850s.

Self-description

Fitting but not unusual names were appended to other valley areas: Oak Grove, Pine Grove, Middle Valley, Parkdale, Green Point, Dead Point, the latter describing a burned-off section in the hills.

Other self-descriptive tags: Trout, Mill, Indian, Spring and Eagle creeks; Middle, Shell Rock and Wind mountains; Rainy Badger, Black, Blue, Frog and North lakes, to mention a few.

The branches of the Hood river which flow out of Mount Hood glaciers were given good, plain names about which there could be little question: East, Middle, West forks and Lake branch.

The most colorful names came from the Indians: Polallie creek, "sand land"; Wahkeena falls, "most beautiful"; WahGwinGwin falls, "tumbling water"; Wahtum lake, "water lake"; Multnomah, an Indian tribal name believed to have meant "down river."

"Wah" appears in many Indian place-names and means "water," it is thought.

Touch of humor

Someone showed a spark of humor when they called three consecutive streams flowing into the East fork of the Hood river Dog river, Puppy creek and Cat creek.

Wind spot

VIENTO – A former railroad point west of Hood River, now a campground. Two theories exist: 1 "Viento," Spanish for "wind," 2 The first letters in the names of three men involved in the building of the railroad – Villard, Endicott and Toman. Those who have picnicked at Viento on a windy day will accept the first theory.

Highest peak

MOUNT DEFIANCE – A 4,960-foot "recent" volcano on the northwest side of Hood River Valley. Named by Dr. P.G. Barrett because of its "defiance" of the seasons in clinging longest to winter snows. It is the highest peak in the Gorge region.

Party not lost

LOST LAKE – Thought to have been named by the first party of Hood River men who set out to find it after they had seen the blue lake from the slopes of Mount Hood. It was difficult to reach and the going was bad. A native saying, "Indian not lost – wigwam lost," furnished inspiration for the name, according to members of the local explorers' group.

GOVERNMENT CAMP – Now part of the Mount Hood ski area on the south side of the mountain. When the 1st U.S. Mounted Rifles crossed Mount Hood by the Barlow road late in 1849, they lost most of their animals and abandoned 45 wagons to the winter weather at that point, which was 3,888 feet high.

Englisher Mountain

MOUNT HOOD – Named for Rear Admiral Samuel Hood, British Admiralty officer, by Lt. W.R. Broughton, who first saw the snowcap in October, 1792. It was called Wy'east or Wy'am by the Indians.

COLUMBIA RIVER – The name of Capt. Robert Grey's American vessel which sailed over the bar at the mouth of the river May 11, 1792, and which he applied to the great body of water.

BRIDGE OF THE GODS – Name of the interstate span at Cascade Locks. Indian legends spoke of a natural arch over the Columbia at this point. The tale was immortalized in a famous novel, "The Bridge of the Gods" by Frederick Homer Balch, a young Congregational minister who lived and preached in Hood River.

Geologists favor the theory of a great landslide from the north which pushed the river out of its natural channel and strewed basalt blocks to form the treacherous rapids and cascades in the river, later covered by the water behind Bonneville Dam.

The Great Shute

CASCADE LOCKS – The site of locks built in 1896 by the federal government to move boats safely past the "Great Shute," as Lewis and Clark called the rapids at this point. The locks may still be seen.

CLOUD CAP INN – One of the few imaginative names in the area, given to a guest lodge built in 1889 high on the north side of Mount Hood. It closed in the 1920s, but the building still stands at one of the most spectacular viewpoints in the Cascades.

WHITE SALMON – The origin of this name for river and town opposite Hood River has never been settled. It has probably evolved from an Indian legend, for the mouth of the White Salmon river has been a native fishing ground for generations.

BINGEN – Named by Mr. Suksdorf, a native of Germany, who came to the area in 1874. Approaching the village, he remarked that it reminded him of Bingen-on-the Rhine. His son was Wilhelm Suksdorf, one of the Northwest's six famous early botanists.

April 18, 1968

— ❧ —

LOCATION, LOCATION, LOCATION

The site of the new valley high school is splendid even at this drab time of year. In all four directions it shows off our gem of a valley and all the mountains which form our fruit bowl. The Westside school location is no less handsome.

Lawrence Perkins, Chicago architect specializing in school design, would approve. Interviewed last year in Portland, he remarked that in such beautiful natural settings as we have in Oregon, schools should take advantage of the marvelous outlook.

"Blend the outdoors with your school structures," he advised. "Make this beauty part of the children's education and you will be giving them a priceless gift which will enrich their lives."

Nov. 28, 1968

— ❧ —

FRUIT FROM HOME

From Teunis Wyers, Jr., back home in new London, Connecticut, from his third Polaris patrol aboard the nuclear submarine John Marshall:

> ... when the ship returns from two months of continual submergence, one of the first orders of business is to stalk up on fresh milk, vegetables and fruit; it is a welcome relief from the rehydrated dehydrated diet we live on after the fresh food runs out.
>
> One of the first items to come down the hatch was a nice big case of Diamond Fruit D'Anjou pears! This was in Holy Lock, Scotland, half way around the world from good old Hood River! I was ecstatic. I ate several and offered them to everyone in sight, boasting about their place of origin. A heart-felt thanks DFG and Hood River from the U.S. Submarine Service! It seems that I recall a similar occurrence in Vietnam, and the grower and packer were traced from the numbers on the box, so I copied these numbers with the hopes that this could be done again.

Jan. 29, 1970

— ❧ —

GOT A QUESTION: HERE'S AN ANSWER

Answers to questions often asked by visitors to Hood River Valley:

Why is the town of Hood River built on a steep hill?

Because the hill was there in the first place, silly! All major transportation in and out of the valley is along the Columbia river, so the town naturally sprang up at that point.

Has the Columbia river been used for anything but barges and pleasure boats?

Steamboats, the old paddlewheelers, were the public means of travel through the Columbia gorge until the first railroad was built in 1882. The old stern and sidewheelers remained in regular use until the Columbia River highway was completed in 1915-16.

When was Hood River settled?

The first permanent white settlers arrived in 1854. Four Donation Land Claims were taken out: on the present site of the town, to the east and west of it, and one on Indian creek to the south.

Have the dams on the Columbia changed Hood River's waterfront?

Yes. When Bonneville dam was completed in 1938, the lake behind it drastically altered the Columbia shoreline. Until that time beaches, sandbars and islands abounded, with thick groves of cottonwoods and willows extending out into the sand.

Is Hood River a good area for Indian artifacts?

No. Very little of previous cultures has been found here, except arrowheads. The "fish-eating" Chinook tribes here produced nothing but the most primitive implements. Arrowheads were once plentiful on the sandbars, especially at the mouth of the Hood river.

What's so great about Koberg's beach?

This riverside area is a mere shadow of the mid-Columbia's only fine, large beach in pre-Bonneville dam years. It had a stone pavilion for dancing, an excellent cove for swimming, diving boards, bath houses and a big area under the cottonwoods for picnics. A bus from Hood River took youngsters to Koberg's for supervised swim lessons.

Are there any covered bridges?

Not today, although several were in use until the 1950s.

Where is the best fishing?

This area is blessed with year-around sport for the angler. Trout are waiting for bait or fly in the Hood river and its east fork. Neal creek, Lake branch also have them. The high lakes are good – Lost, Rainy, Wahtum and Green Point reservoir.

Steelhead averaging 7 to 8 pounds, and once in a while up to 20, are in the Hood river for winter and spring spawning. Sturgeon fishing is off rocky points along the Columbia and from the old locks at Cascade Locks. The prize might be 3 to 6 feet long.

Most spring and fall salmon are caught from trolling boats off the mouth of the White Salmon and Klickitat rivers on the Washington side of the Columbia. A few enter the Hood river.

In the sloughs and backwater lakes of the Columbia there are plenty of spiny ray fish, black bass, crappies and catfish, if you know how to catch them.

How big is Mount Hood?

Claimed by Portland but actually Hood River Valley's private property, Mount Hood is 11,235 feet, making it the highest mountain in Oregon.

April 23, 1969 Vacationer, Hood River News

— ○ℜ —

WHISKY CREEK NAME REMAINS

Over the years, residents of the Pine Grove area tried to erase the stigma of Whisky creek's name by calling the short road which borders it something else.

State highway maps of the 1920s showed the official name as "Pine Grove Market road," but locally it was still "Whisky Creek road."

In 1928, Grangers petitioned the county court for a change to "Pomona Market road." Today it is still "Whisky Creek road," the trickle of water said to have been named for an applejack operation near its source.

1971 Panorama, Hood River News

— ❧ —

MAGIC NAME OVERUSED

The name "Hood River" was so widely associated with fine quality because of its fruit after 1900 that unscrupulous merchants took advantage of the magic label.

A Hood River man visiting Seattle in 1904 saw this sign in a grocery window – "Fresh Hood River Eggs." Those hen fruits were five cents above the market price, and it was very doubtful they were from this valley.

That same year the Hon. L.N. Blowers came upon a man peddling apples on a Portland street. His sign read "Hood River Apples – 6 for a nickel."

Blowers addressed everyone within earshot. "I lived 15 years in Hood River and I know that these apples never came from there. The farmers of Hood River feed better apples to their hogs!"

The vendor moved on to the next block.

1973 Panorama, Hood River News

— ❧ —

Rockhounds Find Area Geological Youngster

Note to rockhounds: Don't waste your time looking for valuable gemstones in Hood River county. There are none.

By geological age this area is very young. During the "Cascades Revolution" of some 15 million years ago, Mount Hood arose through volcanic eruption. The vulcanism continued until a mere 15,000 or 10,000 years ago, say geologists. That is practically newborn by earth-age standards.

The Hood river and its branches make up a relatively young water system. The valley itself is a structural trough filled with alluvial deposits, andesitic lava flows and glacial deposits far too new to have developed the fine quartz materials found farther east in the state.

Surrounding mountains are not much older.

No valuable gems nor metals are found to any extent in the county, aside from occasional jaspagnates [sic] in stream beds. A few petrified wood finds were made in earlier days, but these are now exhausted.

Nor will the Indian artifact collector want to tarry here.

Arrowheads were a dime a dozen at the mouth of the Hood river in earlier times. A number of Indian tools used to be found, especially around Cascade Locks, an ancient village site.

Most of the "digs" are now covered by water impounded behind the big dams.

Columbia river petroglyphs, the primitive carvings incised on cliffs and boulders of the river and having mysterious origins, were largely lost in the dam backwaters.

By a wax negative process, many carvings were documented before their loss, with absolute fidelity for preservation.

A very few pictographs remain along the river.

1974 Panorama, Hood River News

NEITHER INDIAN NOR CHICKEN

A letter from Portland, in part:

> ... Before the Kennedys built on "Chicken Charlie's
> Island," there were the remains of an old weathered
> house or cabin. Could this have been where the
> Indian Charlie lived? ... Mr. and Mrs. T.R.K.

As for the 15-acre island close to Mosier, it has been known since early days as Eighteen Mile Island 18 miles downstream from The Dalles. In 1900, G.R. French lived there and raised chickens. So "Chicken Island" came about. It has also been called "Goat Island."

In later years the little old house on the island was occupied by Charlie Reither, who was neither an Indian nor a chicken. But he was a recluse, only leaving his windy fortress by row boat to get water and staples in Mosier.

Once in a while he rowed down to Hood River and walked to the Heights to buy a certain course meal of which he was fond.

Otherwise, he stayed on his island within sight of his old home at Bingen, Wash. He welcomed neither pleasure boats, fishermen nor hunters around his island. Especially not hunters, for he loved the wild fowl on his preserve.

Someone cared about Charlie. The crew of a west-bound night train always looked for his lantern light dimly seen in the shack. If it was not lit, they left word at the station and someone would go up the next day to check on Charlie.

The night came in 1964 when Eighteen Mile Island was a black huddle in the Columbia. Charlie had died.

HOOD RIVER GETS AROUND

Hood River products do get around the world. Homeward bound after two years teaching in Australia, Lin Miller spotted Diamond

Fruit apples in Shanghai markets. On a flight to Bangkok she was served — you guessed it — Hood River apple juice. *Jan. 13, 1977*

—⊗—

Notes from the Margin

Oops! Someone's directions are mixed. Our geography teacher hated her fourth grade student. Lin Miller was NOT in Shanghai. Hood River apples are not welcome in Red China. She saw them in Singapore markets.

Jan. 27, 1977

—⊗—

Polite Signs

We Americans don't mince words, especially on our public signs. Our state anti-litter sign, "Keep Oregon Green," is closer to European niceties than most.

In England and Scotland you are admonished to "Keep Britain Tidy." In the old Paris flower market, signs read "Please touch with the eyes only."

Where They Live —

the place, the street, the road — is of more concern to people than you realize. The only subject to bring Over the Picket Fence more response was a discussion of coleslaw recipes some years ago.

Margaret (Mrs. John) Piatt, who lives there, asks where Riordan Hill above Post Canyon got its name and what is the correct spelling.

(continued)

Closest guess is that it was named for a George Riordan, a farmer who helped organize the first Lutheran church in a building now a residence near the top of Davidson Hill.

A directory of 1905 lists "George Riorden, 160 acres — 8 apple, 15 hay, balance unimproved." Old church records spell it Riorden. Old papers have it Riordan. Take your choice.

March 10, 1977

— ∞ —

"TO ERR IS HUMAN" ...

so OPF is very human and very humble. Once and for all, it's truly LENZ Butte. Lois Dimmick Morgan ought to know; John Lenz was her grandfather. All those old directories and newspapers and Mount Hood Railroad schedules were wrong. Thank you, Lois.

May 12, 1977

— ∞ —

GET IT RIGHT

Still getting reports of gremlins in the Dept. of County Drive and Road Sign-Making (DCRS-M) and Dept. of County Map-Making (DCM-M).

Sharp-eyed residents out there are irked by the inconsistency of signs in their neighborhood. One at the east end of that awesome road over Lenz Butte says, "Erk Hill." Sign on the Odell side properly reads "Ehrck."

The name is for brothers Charles and Willima Ehrck, who settled there in 1878-79.

June 9, 1977

— ∞ —

LOCAL HIT PARADE?

One of our operatives who loves to shop flea markets and old book stores spotted an extensive display of old sheet music singing the glories of Oregon.

"Dreamy Oregon Moon," "Oregon Rose Time Fox Trot," "Come to Roseland with Me," "Beautiful Oregon I Love You."

He was surprised at the quantity of such numbers, but not at the quality. None of them ever made the Hit Parade.

Among the forgotten music, reported Operative 57, was "The Columbia Highway Waltz," music by Edwin Dicey, words by Edward Thornton.

It was published by Thornton, in Hood River, probably in the early 1920s when the Columbia River Scenic Highway, newly opened, gave local people something to sing about. It was the first decent road out of the valley for automobiles.

June 30, 1977

—❧—

CABIN FEVER …

is what most of us refer to this time of year, but a former HR doctor now practicing on the Oregon coast had another name for it. When folks came in to him in dark January or February with mild depression, vague aches and general debility, he told them they had "winter."

Feb. 23, 1978

—❧—

PRETTIEST PLACE

The name "Hood River" jumps out at local readers from newspapers and magazines.

(continued)

The March 1980 issue of "Farm and Ranch Living" features the grand old August Paasch home on Paasch drive. Titled "The Prettiest Place in the Country," the article describes the residence from facts provided by Allan and Myris Paasch, with photographs of the home and valley scenes.

Early prefab

As never before people want to know the history of older homes they move into in Hood River town and valley. Who built it? When? What was it like originally? Likewise, buildings.

One couple whose small home is now the counterpart of an efficient modern apartment knew that, before being completely renovated by the late Dayton McLucas, it was a square box of a house built around 1900.

They have learned that many similar houses were produced around the turn of the century by Sears Roebuck in the east and shipped out by rail. They were actually the forerunners of today's prefabricated structures.

An ugly town?

... which recalls a frank statement in a promotional brochure meant to lure newcomers shortly after the turn of the century.

"Hold up your opinion of Hood River Valley until after you see it. You cannot see the valley from the train. Don't judge the valley from the town. We are just as ashamed of the town as you are. But the streets are to be paved this summer and the city made beautiful."

Feb. 14, 1980

— ‿ —

THEY KEEP COMING BACK —

those who went to the old HRHS where May Street School is now, or to the "new" HRHS, presently the Hood River Junior High.

Two groups of four classes who lived through the thorny Twenties and early Depression, 1925-1932, will be in town this weekend for reunions. We welcome them back to the place they remember with some fondness. Those who have no pleasant memories of Hood River in their youth won't be here anyway.

There will be good-natured banter and apt quotes:

"Same old faces but more new teeth!"

"I never had an identity crisis. When I was a kid I was told who I was and that was that."

"I don't mind telling my age. I just mind being it."

There will be recall:

"Remember when having climbed Mount Hood was a status symbol? I carry a card proving that I made it up during a Legion climb."

"I see the HR News is still being published. I remember all those years the Scotsman, Hugh Ball, was editor. He used to sit down at a linotype and cast his editorials hot off the cuff."

"They've made our swamp into a park. How do kids get initiated these days if there's no cruddy swamp to throw them in?"

"Used to play football in the snow – Redd Acheson, Willard Jarvis, Brick Stratton, John Boyd, Tommy Swanson, the Mendenhalls. Never minded bad weather. A street scraper would clear off the snow before a game."

(continued)

"I stood in the dining room of the Hood River Inn and thought of Homer Van Allen's ferry docking right there practically on that spot."

"In my day a heavy date was driving towards The Dalles on the old highway and pulling off to drink hard cider. It only had about one-half percent kick to it."

"One Saturday night at a dance in Koberg's Pavilion my date thought it would be a big deal to go up the river with Bill Wright to check his fish net. There I was in my best dress, sitting in a small boat out in the pitch-black Columbia while Bill pulled in a great big salmon and whacked its head over the gunwale. We smelled of fish so we couldn't go back to the dance. Was I mad!"

"My folks used to tell about the time long ago when the barbershop was called the Bon Ton and had bathing rooms because most people didn't have plumbing in their homes. It seems a cleaning woman working on the upper floor fell through a skylight right over the Bon Ton one day. She got stuck between floors but the shower of glass and the sight of her feet dangling from the ceiling sent bathers out into the street stark naked."

"I'm paraphrasing some writer but I say that the most beautiful road in the world is from Hood River to Portland and the second most beautiful is the road back to Hood River!"

July 17, 1980

— ℂℜ —

"WORLD'S LARGEST MUSICAL INSTRUMENT"

Our interstate bridge was dubbed on Friday, Sept. 5, during NBC's "Today" show.

In a pleasantly long, tongue-in-cheek segment put together by Jon Tuttle of Channel 8, Portland, the whole country saw and heard the "singing bridge," as this family has always called it, on which a vehicle can play a tune by varying speed as it passes over the metal plates.

Tuttle's segment played "Happy Birthday" by patching in the sound of traffic passing across our bridge. It created a recognizable melody with only a B-flat missing from the scale.

Sept. 11, 1980

—CR—

WELCOME WIND

Most welcome so far in 1984 — the Chinook wind arriving to nibble at the ice and snow crust.

The warming southwest wind got its name, according to historians, in early Astoria. Many Indians of the Chinook Tribe lived along the coastline and every camp had kitchen middens piled high with shells and refuse from their fish-eating diet.

When that warmer, welcome breeze blew across those garbage heaps and on to Astoria after a cold winter spell, it wafted an unmistakable and unpleasant fishy odor to that settlement. Hence, the "Chinook" wind.

Feb. 8, 1984

—CR—

LEST WE FORGET NATURAL WONDERS ...

in the Columbia Gorge which were here even before we were, Geologist John Eliot Allen points them out in "The Magnificent Gateway."

"Possibly the greatest concentration of high waterfalls in North America appear on the south walls of the gorge ... twenty-five falls

(continued)

are well enough known to be mapped, and 11 over 100 feet high can be seen from the freeway or scenic highway. Another 13 lie from 2 to 7 miles up the canyons."

And a complaint about the drive from Portland to Hood River. Visitors long familiar with it remark that trees and brush allowed to grow between the freeway and the river almost completely obliterate the Columbia view.

Aug. 9, 1989

— CR —

AUTUMN SOUNDS AND SMELL ...

of Hood River town have changed. No more truckloads of fruit bins rumbling down to storage and processing plants near the railroad tracks. None of that spicy fragrance of apples floating over the town, or did we just imagine it?

And surely, when the vinegar plant and the cannery were operating, their odors could be identified. Now that fruit operations are located out in the valley, it is easy to forget our big industry, 90-or-so years old.

One man did not forget! Lesley Forden, HRHS class of 1932, drove non-stop from Alameda, Calif., to Portland, then to Hood River "to hear the trucks rumbling, and to smell autumn in the valley." He was only here overnight.

Oct. 20, 1990

— CR —

HISTORIC HIGHWAY BEGINNING RECALLED

Anyone in Hood River who recalls the thrilling days when the first Columbia River Highway was the only way to get by car to Portland will appreciate this weekend's celebration of the road's 75 years. Completion of the route, although still unpaved in 1915, brought this town into the automobile world.

The original road was built in a time before heavy equipment when the highway was literally constructed by hand. The late, famous Mitchell Point tunnel was blasted out of solid basalt, the rubble carried away by wheelbarrow.

Towns like Cascade Locks and Hood River were responsible for clearing their own approaches. On a Saturday in 1915, Hood River businessmen and farmers hacked away brush along the old cowpath from Ruthton Hill to Mitchell Point, moving dirt and building a retaining wall. Wives provided meals. By Sunday night there was a passable way to the tunnel.

Not all highway plans worked out. One proposal was to pipe organ music down the sides of Crown Point, "to stimulate wind through the evergreens." It was found that the continuous gale across the point made its own music.

In those days of open cars, as an auto neared Crown Point, each passenger took a tight hold on the wood ribs of the canvas top, to keep it from sailing away.

Said by those who remember: "Sometimes it was so windy up there you had to crawl into the marble Vista House on your hands and knees." There is no sign that the wind has abated since then.

Of the original Columbia River Highway left to travel, some of its marvels of construction remain, unused and hidden. The Moffet Bridge, now almost unseen, was a beauty, said to be the longest three-hinge concrete bridge in the world in 1915, built at a cost of $16,390.59. Its graceful, arched 170 feet rises only 17 feet over the creek.

Hood River was only a two-and-a-half hour trip from Portland on the old highway, if you drove the 24-foot-wide road very carefully.

June 15, 1991

— CR —

CHAPTER 3

BIRDS OF A FEATHER

— and other fascinations of nature

Earth Rebirth

And so the sun comes out, the warmth creeps down among last year's leaves and you get on your hands and knees to uncover the forgotten primrose, thinking that this tonic beats sulfur and molasses all hollow. Or, if you don't, you've missed the good, quickening pulse of the earth as it rolls from winter into spring.

March 26, 1954

— ❧ —

Getting the Mad Out

Take it from the voice of experience: The best way to get rid of mental aches and pains is to bury them two feet deep out in the good old earth. Scratching a red-hot mad into the garden or throwing a worry into the weedpile is very therapeutic.

April 30, 1954

Birds' Menu

Slim pickings for birds when it snows. If you've enjoyed their company the rest of the year, here's your chance to repay. Considering their numbers, winter birds do more good in the garden than those of the summer.

Here's a general bird menu suggested by an authority: Suet, canary seeds, chopped peanuts and raisins, oatmeal, sunflower seeds, cooked and uncooked rice, honey, sugar, cornmeal, coarse bran, lettuce and cabbage leaves, celery tops, hard-boiled eggs, chopped apples.

Especially for our juncos and sparrows: Wild bird seed, pounded-up dog biscuits, chick feed, bread crumbs mixed with grease and crumbled-up corn bread.

For the chickadees and jays: Spread peanut butter thickly on branches. They'll love you for it.

(continued)

An important item; Don't forget to put sand or coal ashes in the bird feeder, to aid their little digestive processes in snowtime.

Jan. 14, 1955

— ⅍ —

BIRD TALES

BB brigade

Those starlings better not try this neighborhood. We've organized a whole brigade of young hunters on the business end of BB guns and they're alerted for action, now that we understand it's all legal.

Symbolic freedom

Bird watching takes patience and time, but it is rewarding.

As Roger Tory Peterson puts it so well, "Birds can fly where they want to when they want to. So it seems to us, who are earthbound. They symbolize a degree of freedom that we would nearly give our souls to have. Perhaps this is why bird watching has almost become a national hobby in Britain and is rapidly becoming one here. It is an antidote for the disillusionment of today's world."

Birds have issues, too

Eunice Coryell likes birds — in their proper place. Which isn't knocking themselves out against her windowpane.

"Monotonous!" she opined of a robin who'd been rapping on the glass all one day last week. She even tried frightening him with the vacuum cleaner. He didn't budge. In fact he came back at breakfast time for days.

Bird authorities tell us that he apparently is suffering from a narcissistic complex. Just loves to look at himself. Eunice has another theory. She thinks he's the reincarnation of a frustrated window peeper!

March 25, 1955

— ᖇ —

FANCY'S FATE

The ways of wild birds are strange and wonderful. A bird of the forest in grateful captivity is even more fascinating.

Several years ago the Runckel boys found a cedar waxwing badly injured. They gave it to Dorothy and Barbara Parsons, knowing their charmed way with birds and animals.

A doctor diagnosed the waxwing's injury as a dislocated shoulder. With affection and care, the bird was soon back in bouncing good health, thriving the year around on a diet of chopped apple, and the addition of small red berries in the summer.

From the first, "Fancy" made himself at home with the Parsons, growing larger and plumper than his wild brethren, and loving his cage. Mrs. Parsons perched him on the clothesline when she was busy in the yard and Fancy showed no disposition to leave, although he could fly in a limited way.

This summer, the family was called to California, leaving their beautiful fawn-gray bird, two canaries, two parakeets, a chameleon and numerous cats in the care of a dependable boy. During their absence Fancy began to fail. He lost interest in his menu, except for a little hand-feeding.

When the Parsons returned, it was too late. Fancy was thin and listless, and even the coming of the little red berries he loved so well could not rouse him. Two days later he died, and anyone who understands the strange attachment of a bird for its protectors will agree that the cause was a broken heart.

July 29, 1955

— ᖇ —

Bird IQ

For two summers we have watched a violet green swallow who elected to raise her broods behind a kitchen ventilator. The wonder is not so much how she has avoided the unpredictable blades of the fan ... but how in the world has she taught the little ones to stay in their 3 -1/2-inch space behind it? So far as is known, neither broods of three ever suffered a casualty. And you say birds are dumb?

Sept. 23, 1955

— ℭℜ —

Bird nest art

Soon comes the time for the seeking of bird nests when the departure of leaves exposes their hiding places. And what skillful little structures most of them are!

Neighbor brings a tiny, compact cup from an apple tree — hundreds of rootlets painstakingly interwoven and lined with horsehair. Another friend saves us a two-inch thick carpet of moss, bits of wool and human hair laid in her birdhouse by a pair of chickadees. From the Willamette Valley we treasure the seven-inch hanging home of a coast bushtit.

As others admire the skill of the glassblower or the potter so a birder sees in the nest an art more beautiful and a workmanship more mysterious than the handicraft of man.

Oct. 21, 1955

— ℭℜ —

Statistical quandry

Averages are sometimes deceiving. A western garden book gives the average date of killing frost in Hood River as October 20. In a community of such elastic altitudes, where would that average be ... top or bottom of Booth hill, mayhap?

Oct. 28, 1955

— ᏼ —

Happy New Year!

The break between jaded summer and cracker-crisp autumn is physically nearer a complete dividing line in the year than Jan. 1. The frazzled countryside changes its costume quickly from that point on. Color shifts from the fading fields to the trees, as leaves take their turn at the paintpots.

The irritations of the past season die away along with the itching of mosquito bites. The air is quiet on some days, so quiet that seedpods of the weeds may be heard popping open as they sew next season's crop. Bees are giddy with their harvest, staggering from salvia to sunflower.

The approach of autumn is the shadow of birds passing overhead. Out in the valley it is not the traditional formations alerting us to the season so much as the quick, quiet passage of a single western tanager and the plaintive, piercing demands of young goldfinches being beak-fed in the nut tree.

Yes, September is the start of a new year, when we cast an uneasy eye at the raingutter full of summer debris, put away desultory habits with the swim suits and swear that things are going to be very different — and better — from now on.

Sept. 3, 1959

— ᏼ —

Chipmunk parenting 101

Ol' Auntie Remus going to tell a story about the little animal folks, so just you growed-ups skedaddle back to TV whilst we younguns talk about the latest happenstance out in the forest.

(continued)

Folks from Hood River had an outing way up on Mount Hood this past summer. Soon found they had a caller, a beady-eyed li'l old chipmunk who sat on a certain stump and watched them.

This wasn't all. Every time it scampered away on chipmunk business, three li'l heads popped out from under a root of the stump and six teeny-weeny eyes stared at the campers.

Well, from this the camper judged that the chipmunk on the stump was the mama, and the three under the stump were her chillun. And it was plain to see that those chillun had orders not to stare at strangers, cause the only time they popped out was when mama went away.

This went on a spell until, like all chillun, they got caught breakin' the house rules. Without an ah, yes, or no, Mrs. Chipmunk took her chipmunk babies one at a time, rolled them into tight little balls and carted them off to a new house, away from human campers.

You see, forest mamas don't go for their younguns breakin' the family rules, and so they raise some might obedient chillun, which should be a lesson to us humans.

Next week Ol' Auntie Remus goin' to tell you about a kitten that taught its mama a lesson.

Oct. 20, 1960

— ○ℛ —

KITTEN TEACHES MOM A THING OR TWO

Ol' Auntie Remus goin' to tell a close-to-home story. Two ladies, names of Mrs. Eby and Mrs. Goyette, share a cat. Now, how do you half-and-half a cat, pray! And this cat has kitties. Don't know who gets THEM.

One day something scared Mrs. Cat and family. The kitties took off for an ol' skunk hole. Their mama scampered onto a roof and into a tree. When the kitties came up, glory be! Mrs. Cat was in the tree howlin' and carryin' on something fierce. Seems she'd got herself going the wrong way on a limb that didn't go anywhere.

Well, one li'l feller couldn't stand it. He or she, as the case may be — and I'll bet I know which it was — climbed up that tree and gave its mama some instructions in its special kitty language, then backed down the treetrunk again slow and easy, as if to say, "See Mom? This is the way to do it."

Mrs. Cat thought it over, backed off her perch and came down the tree tail-first and careful, just like her baby showed her.

Now Mrs. Goyette saw this happen and we don't doubt her for even a little minute because she was a teacher and teachers tell the truth as they see it.

Oct. 27, 1960

— ❧ —

SNOWBIRD FEAST

Arrival of the white-crowned sparrows back on the lawn last week prompts us to dig out this oldie from a long-past Picket column:

> Snowbird, snowbird, where do you
> come from?
> What high-up cold in the hills
> do you run from?
> I saved my nicest, my meatiest
> Seeds for you …
> I am the gardener with the
> mostest weeds for you!

Oct. 12, 1961

— ❧ —

HERE CLEO, CLEO, CLEO

Like the camel with his nose in the tent, Cleo the Downtown Hound is slyly taking over the business area. She drags her under-slung chassis diagonally across an intersection at the busiest time. Traffic waits.

(continued)

She selects a shaded or sunny metered spot, according to the weather, and sleeps in it without putting in a penny. Parked well out in the street, she lies so that no driver would dream of trying to squeeze in around her. She leads a charmed life.

At least, she did. Here Cleo! Here Cleo! Anyone seen Cleo lately?

Oct. 10, 1963

— CR —

FLIGHT LESSON

If anyone else had reported this bird story, we'd not believe them. But this was Nell Allen, C of C secretary, and Nell doesn't imagine such things. The Allens have a nice, peaceful yard for birds, a house finch couple (those blithe singers with the males sporting a flashy strawberry front) preempted a good branch for their house building. When the nestlings began to stir and flutter their wings, Nell saw what we have never heard or read about. The mother went to the nest. One precocious youngster climbed aboard her back and off they flew, The young bird instinctively spread his wings for flight just like mama. On the approach to a limb some 15 feet away, the adult finch dropped out from under her passenger, who flew onto the landing point under its own power. Now, Nell saw it happen so we believe her.

May 28, 1964

— CR —

HAPPY HUMMINGBIRD

For a final true bird story, this one is hard to believe. One of the hummingbirds which the Lloyd Gilkersons of Odell regularly feed in the summer refused to go off to Mexico this winter. Isabel worried about it, even put a light in the outdoor feeder lying on the snow. Brought in, warmed and fed its regular sugar-water, the hummer has made a complete recovery and now lives in a box among flowers and limbs for perching. Happy as a clam, too, the Gilkersons report.

Jan. 23, 1966

—CR—

GROUSE MEET-AND-GREET, PART 1

Now that the tumult has died and the voting's over, let's get back to chitchat. It gives one an almost perverse pleasure to consider little, local things again, at a time when the national trend is toward the enormous, the expensive, the expansive, the Most.

Last week, driving up the Old Dalles road, we met a bird. He walked downhill to meet us. We stopped. He was a dusky grouse. Since grouse are the most unwary of all wild fowl, he walked the length of the car, eyeing us in a friendly way. We got out and crouched down beside him.

"Good evening!"

"Awk – awkawka wk!" He went around to the driver's side with the same greeting, then back. We carried on a cozy conversation within 15 inches of each other and it might have continued until dark. He seemed willing but we had to leave.

May 26, 1966

—CR—

IRIS WEATHER VANE

Better than weathermen to forecast June winds, just watch when the tall iris blooms. Cliff Wells, Grace Carter and other fanciers of this most majestic flower have almost given up their hybridizing and extensive cultivation of the tall bearded varieties. As soon as they burst into blossom, the wind and/or rain come.

Grouse meet-and-greet, part 2

Kathleen and Dick Nichols met the same grouse we mentioned earlier, presumably at the same place in the Old Dalles road, and found him just as friendly as ever. In fact, they petted him. A few days later they could find no grouse.

The Nichols also glimpsed a wild turkey, which we at first assumed to be a bird who hated Thanksgiving and left home, then learned a few families of the birds were released there by the state game commission.

June 9, 1966

—ೞ—

Lullaby of the traffic

Now that trees are denuded, the discovery of deserted nests close to streets and highways indicates that birds like the lullaby of traffic. Note particularly the many nests in trees along the Banfield freeway outside Portland city limits. Ruth Blackburn reports seeing not one but two of those great pileated woodpeckers, which scarcely anyone can view or hear without a kind of excitement. These birds were almost done in by the Indians, who valued their red heads, but an early ornithologist stated ironically that since the Indian was becoming extinct, the woodpecker was coming back. And it was true!

Speeding ticket

And then, there is the Hood River Valley lady who was arrested early in the 1900s on Twelfth street by the town marshal for "speeding" on her horse. It was a mere trot, but the fine was $25, within $2.50 of being half her month's salary.

Humiliated and furious, she headed her horse toward home at a fast clip and the marshal thereupon threatened to fine her another $25, again for speeding. The "arrest" didn't stick but this fine, law-abiding lady has had to live with her "offense" all these years and so we wouldn't tell her name for anything. She's afraid her friends might misunderstand, which we doubt. You just better believe she still drives through town CAREFULLY.

Nov. 7, 1968

— ☞ —

During one of the worst winters

Back in the Twenties the Oregonian ran a small story which was picked up around the world. It claimed that ring-necked or China pheasants in Hood River Valley had been seen sitting on apples in the orchards to thaw them out for eating.

Feb. 10, 1977

— ☞ —

The true "environmentalist" ...

is exemplified by a local man who waited to start an outside carpentry job on his house until a pair of robins had topped off the hatching and rearing of two nestlings so close by that they would probably have abandoned the eggs if he had gone ahead with the work.

The fact that there were only two eggs ties in with other reports of smaller families among resident robins in recent years. It is claimed that poisons of various kinds in our environment are resulting in soft-shelled bird eggs which don't survive the incubation period.

May 26, 1977

— ☞ —

A mini-struggle for survival ...

was won in the George Alexanders' back yard.

(continued)

Peking ducks belonging to the Alexanders have not had great luck nesting. Their enemies, probably animals living along Phelps Creek, have taken the eggs; a laying female was devoured.

One mother-to-be figured a way to beat the odds. Some four feet up in a huge oak she found a notch ready-lined with leaves. Now, it isn't easy for a domestic duck to climb a tree but this one geared up her clumsy wings, made a run for it and, adapting her webbed feet, somehow scrambled up to her new apartment.

Her eggs threatened to overflow the narrow space. Mrs. Alexander let her keep seven and Mrs. Duck slipped in one more, just for good luck. The sight of a white duck nesting in an oak tree took visitors back.

And she did it — hatched her lovely ducklings who, at last report, were enjoying the Alexander pond.

May 31, 1979

— ෬ —

Bird inventory

If statistics were available you'd be amazed at the number of people in Hood River Valley who fed wild birds last month. Stores couldn't keep chick scratch in stock. Bird seed went out at a fast clip. Day-old bread, too.

I thank you for all of the birds still alive today because so many cared and shoveled snow and hacked at the ice to keep feedlots clear.

The 16 species seen on one small cleared place in the heart of Hood River: English, song, white-crowned, gold-crowned and Harris sparrows; finches, evening grosbeaks, California and Stellar's jays, cedar waxwings, starlings, chickadees, nuthatches, Northwest flickers, towhees and at least three junco subspecies.

Out in the country, people faithfully fed China pheasants and flocks of quail as best they could, rigged up extra feeders, spread grain in every available sheltered spot. It was a heroic effort.

Feb. 14, 1980

— ଔ —

A BUTTERFLY HATCHERY IN THEIR OWN BACKYARD!

Monarch butterflies were sighted outside a Hood River Distillers' door from which wafted the aroma of Monarch — a brand of spirits. What a coincidence, as you read in a recent HR News.

In late July the distillery staff watched the whole process as caterpillars emerged where northbound females had deposited the eggs on the underside of butterfly milkweeds growing in a fenced enclosure to the building. Bob Kirkwood took pictures of the birthing.

Fattened on the leaves, and now green banded with yellow and black stripes, the caterpillar larvae set out across a rocky area to the wire fence, some even up the metal steps of the holding tanks. Once properly settled, the pupa spun a rosette of silk to which it glued its tail as it dangled head down.

In about 24 hours the skin split, showing the chrysalis which hung eight to 12 days before cracking open so that the adult monarch butterfly could struggle out, rest while its body hardened, wings expanded and dried.

After getting their bearings, this last generation of 1982 monarchs headed for Canada, where it will band with the rest of migrants to head south for the winter. The round trip is an estimated 2,000 miles at 25 miles per hour, even with a headwind.

This event at the distillery reminded Ned Marshall of a time when he saw a multitude of monarchs pass over the summit of Mount Hood, where he happened to be standing.

Aug. 25, 1982

— ଔ —

SHEEP IN HOOD RIVER?

Sisters who grew up here, Ann Keller and Pauline Windell of Vancouver, Wash., ask to have a family disagreement settled. Were sheep herded through Hood River as late as the 1920s?

Yes, remembers a woman who saw great flocks driven across the Hood River bridge from the dock at the present site of Hood River Village. They had been landed there from Eastern Oregon, to be taken up the main streets to summer pasture in the west hills. In earlier times, steamers unloaded them at Mitchell Point, from where they spread south to meadowlands.

March 23, 1966

— CR —

BIRD NEWS

Reports an employee of the Inn at Hood River Village Resort, an eagle has hovered now and then above the dining area during Arctic spells. It appeared to be considering three very small ducklings paddling close to shore. Our bird authority notes that a lone eagle has been seen here in other years, during wintry weather.

Glad to have birders in town and valley reporting fairly good-size coveys of quail, which they faithfully feed.

Since it was reported that Barbara Bush used to wear a bathrobe while walking her dog early mornings, we feel less apologetic feeding the birds at that time, in like attire.

March 8, 1989

— CR —

Pondering Nature Through the Years

Raspberries

Oh!
raspberries fat. . .
I have
    eaten
every one picked into
my hat

— ⌘ —

Harvest time

They say, "You're spending too much time
With seed and weed, bonemeal and lime,
You ought to be at the bridge table
Instead of with a silly vegetable!"
But when it comes high time to eat
The garden-fresh and luscious treat

From vine and root, they're glad to share
Your melons, corn and carrots fair,
For then they say, "Now aren't you clever?
Things grow for you with no care whatsoever!"

— ⌘ —

Soup's on

Kind of glad I didn't weed
Nor fight the aphids where they breed,
For now I have a harvest of
Migrating birds, the finch and dove,
Sparrows in their changing feather,
Vireo and chickadee together.
Even blackbirds love my grubby lawn
For the pests they find thereon;

(continued)

All feathered aeronauts arrive
For food a cleaner garden can't provide,
And tiny, grateful sounds proclaim
Thanks for my "Careless Gardener" fame.

— ∞ —

And please don't bother to return them

Neighbor dear, I'm glad to share
    The beauty of my trees in Autumn hue,
And when the leaves let go up there
    I'll gladly let them fall on you!

— ∞ —

Wonders of nature

On a gusty bough a chickadee
    In an August wind sang on,
And the miracle of it all was this —
    How did he hang on?

— ∞ —

Weather story

This year's arrival of a chizzly fall
    Will surprise almost no one at all;
No huddling Hood Riverite apprehends
    Where autumn starts and summer ends.

— ∞ —

No tears for time

Old dog went down by the furnace last night,
    First time he has confessed outright
That the nocturnal chill is too much for his bones …
    And it still September!

Yet he was right. This morning the birds
    Were a different feather, and the calls we heard
Came from flocks setting flight for warmer zones …
    And it still September!

Never mourn Summer with her brazen whims,
　　Autumn comes after, a gold interim,
A time to rest and a time to reap …
　　With much to remember!

The year, brought down to a Winter bed,
　　Spreads a rich coverlet over its head
And Spring is too close for us to weep …
　　With much to remember!

— ❧ —

Undercover work

How doth the pesky gopher do,
　　And all his pesky family, too?
They doeth full well because
　　They dine
On carrots which were to be mine.

I'd just as leave they ate the footsies
　　Off alfalfa and other rootsies,
But weeds for gophers have no
　　Merits …….
They much prefer my tender carits!

— ❧ —

Fair warning

How thoughtless of the neighbor cat
　　Who, full of Kitty Chow and food like that,
Comes burpingly across the yard
　　To stalk the wild birds that I guard.

Beware, fat cat! Be on the run
　　As I reach for my BB gun;
I wouldn't really hit you, on my word —
　　I'd just cool your appetite for bird!

— ❧ —

CHAPTER 4

LOCALS AND NOTABLES

— Famous and fascinating folks

Eph Winans

Eph Winans, the old timer himself, celebrates his 90th birthday Wednesday. What a wonderful [figure] in Hood River, and what colorful memories! First came here in 1886 at the age of 25. Says one reason he stayed was a 10-cent bag of cherries he bought at the depot the day he arrived. Big as plums, they were!

Feb. 18, 1952, Hood River Daily Sun

— ℭℜ —

Percy Manser

Happened on a book published last year which does honor to Percy Manser. It is "Perils on Parnassus" by Wm. F. Alder, an erudite, two-fisted argument against Modernist abstractions.

His thesis: the peril to the fine arts — particularly the art of painting — that exists because of the assault by subversive elements who are trying to infiltrate every phase of American culture with the sole purpose of destroying it …"

Our own Percy Manser enters the picture as one of 10 leading American contemporary artists whose works are reproduced in the book as "true works of art." Mr. Manser's powerful "The Ascents," a massive canvas of three climbers fighting the wind across a high mountain col, takes its place very naturally alongside the work of Dean Cornwall, Hugo Ballin and others.

In a biographical sketch, Mr. Alder says, "To Hood River Valley Percy Manser is every man's painter, one who assembles masterpieces in landscapes with a minimum of strokes, yet attains an effect which all can understand and appreciate." It adds that over 347 Manser paintings are to be found throughout the nation, as well as in several foreign countries. All a glowing, and certainly well-deserved, tribute to Mr. Manser!

April 8, 1955

— ℭℜ —

Hilja Annala

Of some it is said, "They died with all their music in them."

> Not so our friend. She wrote her music in ballads, in sonnets, in gay limericks. She left a large manuscript of ballads, about the valley she loved, the apple orchards and the white mountain. She had a way with words, fitting them together as effortlessly and as beautifully as the petals of a flower are joined.

She possessed a charming quality — the ability to make every friend feel that, above all others, they were dearest to her. A sweet and unforgettable friend she was, indeed.

> Never to walk in the orchard again
>   When Spring conceives the golden fruit?
> Surely she will come back to it then
>   Little singer with her golden lute.
> Piping a song for the northling birds,
>   Singing her valley a ballad of love,
> Weaving April into soundless words
>   About beauty and the goodness thereof.

April 22, 1955

— ∞ —

Peg Jakku

Have to report the "bitter with the better," as Jane Ace used to say. Our Peg Jakku will be laid up for some months after a skiing accident early in January. Suffered a compound fracture and other injuries to one leg, necessitating surgery. She'll be in a cast a long, long time.

But, as we knew they would, Johnny Carpenter, Art Kirkham and the others at KOIN-TV have promised they'll have a sitting-down job for Peg when she's able to come back. And the Portland symphony has said she can come to rehearsals in a wheelchair, if necessary. So life does go on and folks are pretty nice and Peg is not discouraged. All her friends in Hood River send her love and best wishes for a quick recovery.

Jan. 17, 1957

— ❧ —

Dr. W.T. Edmundson, part 1

Dr. W.T. Edmundson is no unfamiliar sight stopping a golf game to crawl on hands and knees along the perimeter of the eighth or ninth greens. He is simply looking for an illusive wildflower which is likely to be only three-eighths of an inch tall.

As a result of his persistent and scientific search over the past couple of years, the good doctor now has identified over 550 Oregon wildflowers.

Sept. 8, 1960

— ❧ —

Dr. W.T. Edmundson, part 2

Years ago a Hood River woman answered the door to find Dr. Eddy there. Without a word he walked in, nodded to another woman and wandered into the kitchen. The women heard the refrigerator door open, pause and then close.

He came back munching on a morsel. "Now, what's the matter?"

"We didn't call you, doctor. We're Christian Scientists."

Wrong address, but he knew where the refrigerator was because he and Mrs. Edmundson had been there for bridge games.

THE SCHERFF GALS

A teen-age music student has inadvertently brought a new innovation to piano recitals. It happened last spring.

Eighth-grader Winetta Scherff was looking for some way to keep her nervous hands from becoming cold and clammy while she waited her turn during the upcoming piano recital. Teacher Lois Talbot suggested soaking them in warm, soapy water.

Winetta, or her mother, had an even better solution. On recital night she arrived with a hotly boiled egg in hand.

As the youngsters sat solemnly awaiting their time at the piano, the egg – still warm and comforting – was held by the one whose solo was next on the program. It was just the ticket to take the coldness, the clamminess out of nimble fingers. It worked wonderfully well.

Teacher later received the egg, handsomely boxed and gift-wrapped as a birthday present and memento of an especially successful recital. Lois has it in her freezer awaiting a future recital. This egg, or a reasonable facsimile, might go on for years as a reminder of the Scherff gals' ingenuity.

June 20, 1963

— ❧ —

"STORMY" KNIGHT

A name mentioned often during the [reunion] weekend was that of the late F.S. Knight, high school principal. He was "Stormy" Knight to the student body, but certainly not to his face.

From thirty-odd years' perspective, what students then interpreted as fear of this silver-haired, ramrod-straight little man is now recognized as respect. He ran a tight ship, taught an excellent course in journalism and supervised the Guide publication.

Meantime, nothing escaped his eagle-keen eyes, his sharp ears or his sensitive nose. He could smell cigarette smoke at 200 paces.

His son Damon became one of the country's most prolific writers of science fiction. A story of his, backed with solid technical data and plenty of imagination, appears in one of the S-F magazines every few months.

Aug. 6, 1964

— ☙ —

CECIL HICKEY

In the food business on the same street for 40 years, Cecil is about to close Hickey's Market on the Heights for good, likely at the end of this month.

And so another of the symbols of small town life disappears — this charge-and-delivery grocery store, as familiar to the homemaker as her own kitchen, where they know the kind of grapefruit you like best and how many chops you'll need, where Mary and Marge and Cecil miss you if you're ill, and you send them postcards from your vacation.

Cecil came to Hood River in 1910 from Swift and Co., worked as a meat cutter for E.J. Young. After service in WW I, he butchered in the Upper Valley, went to Holman and Samuel on the Heights in the late Twenties, then started his own store in the present location with his late wife, Ann.

We'll miss you, Cecil, but it's high time you gave more attention to the ol' golf clubs. For all your satisfied customers we say thanks a million for the years and years of good service.

April 21, 1966

— ☙ —

LASSIE

The last time there was so much excitement over a movie star was when a rumor went around that Clark Gable was eating lunch at the Apple Blossom. He wasn't.

(continued)

With Lassie's visit, collies have upgraded themselves considerably. Our old Jock was begging for dark glasses to wear when he walked downtown, in hopes he'd be taken for the star. No such luck.

Some of the Arnolds are using their raft in front of the HR Village where the Lassie crew is billeted. "Two of them swam out to ask if they could water ski," Jim Arnold said.

"Lassie and his stand-in?" we naturally presumed.

"No, a couple of fellows." Well, anyone who ever watched Lassie on TV wouldn't have been a bit surprised to see the dog water skiing on the Columbia.

Aug. 17, 1967

— ☞ —

Eric Gunderson

Whose face should appear on the back cover of the U of O alumni magazine Old Oregon but that of Eric Gunderson, Oregon sophomore from Hood River.

Eric was shown with a four-foot bridge he built at the University from 1,500 toothpicks as an assignment for a basic design course in architecture. The fragile model held up three and a half bricks, about 14 pounds, before giving away. Eric's only comment on the page which was a plug for the Development Fund, "They made me cut my hair before the picture was taken!" He's really no "long-hair" anyhow; is aiming toward a career in urban planning. His art work is now on view at the county library.

July 10, 1969

— ☞ —

Sasquatch

Legends die hard as recurring reports of the Sasquatch or Bigfoot in Skamania county prove (Panorama '73).

Yet the answer to the mystery is laid out squarely in "The Story of Lige Coalman" for anyone to read. It spoils the lure of the legend but Lige, long-time Mount Hood guide, was a man you could believe.

After leaving our mountain, Lige went to work for the YMCA in Portland. In 1926 he joined the Y staff at the summer camp on Spirit lake, at the base of Mount St. Helens. It was during his years at the camp that one Bigfoot myth originated.

During a camping trip to a flat area on St. Helens' southeast timberline heel, Y boys rolled rocks into a deep gorge leading to a stream which flows into the Lewis river.

Unknown to them, two prospectors lived in the canyon in a lean-to under a rock abutment. When the boulders came rumbling down, close to their shelter, the two men thought the snowcap was becoming unhinged.

Looking upward from the safety of their rock overhang, they saw in the glare of the setting sun what appeared to be eerie creatures cavorting at the head of the canyon far above them.

The peculiar slant of the light elongated arms and legs, turning the perfectly normal Y campers into what the prospectors took to be grotesque creatures invading the mountain.

The two miners, superstitious anyhow, lost no time in hastening to Kelso, Wash., where they told the local newspaper their story of supernatural happenings around Mount St. Helens.

The United Press picked up the tale and sent it around the world. By then the creatures had become ape-men.

Reporters, scientists and tourists created quite a boom for Kelso as they flocked in. Lige thought the truth ought to be told, but YMCA officials hesitated to involve their young campers. Besides, the influx of the curious was good business in Kelso.

According to Lige, the forest rangers knew the truth about the mystery, but they kind of enjoyed the uproar.

(continued)

And now came the crux of Lige's story about the Sasquatch or Bigfoot legend:

> A couple of these rangers immediately set to work preparing huge artificial wooden feet, which they attached to logging boots and snowshoes. It became known that undeniable tracks of the strange furry creatures had been discovered. When this was reported to the rangers, what else could they do but investigate and confirm at the same time that they, themselves, had discovered new tracks … Kelso's practical joke had now gone beyond the point of denial and, so far as I know, this will be the first time the full reliable truth has ever been explained. It is in the undeniable record that very sane and very learned men came to Kelso to investigate, and to spend a little of their time and money there. They and their money were both welcomed.
>
> *May 3, 1973*

Those pioneer promoters who worked so hard to build a reputation for Hood River Valley as the most famous apple and pear basket in the world back in the early 1900s would turn over in their graves if they knew that it is now headquarters for the Bigfoot boom.

Newswire stories out of British Columbia last month appeared all over the country mentioning "the Bigfoot Information Center at Hood River, Ore." OPF received clippings from New Mexico and Ohio.

Maybe this will lead to new fields. We might lay off the fruit industry and grow big feet, instead.

June 7, 1977

— ❧ —

FLORA THOMPSON

Last weekend Flora Thompson, widow of the last chief of the Wy-am tribe at Celilo Falls, came back to Hood River. She has been here before.

"A long time ago I used to pick strawberries here," said the Indian woman no bigger than five minutes. In other days she and Chief Tommy Kuni Thompson had also been guests at the Odell home of Archie and Martha McKeown, photographers, chroniclers and benefactors of the Wy-ams.

Last Saturday Parkdale teacher Elma Rives brought the chief's wife from Celilo to the county library to see the McKeown collection of photographs, many of them of herself and her husband, their tribesmen and their way of life in better days.

On Sunday Mrs. Thompson was guest of honor at Mrs. Rives' home in Parkdale. She wore a buckskin dress of her own making, heavily beaded across the neck and shoulders. Her boots were of a darker buckskin, the color achieved, she said, by smoking the hide.

Over her dark hair, now sprinkled with gray and plaited in braids to her waist, she wore a royal blue kerchief.

Looking at photographs on display at the library, Flora Thompson relived the days when her husband headed the Wy-am tribe through many successful salmon seasons of work, feasting and worship.

She remembered the location of every fishing station at the Falls in any available crevice among the rocks where a platform could be built over the churning water and a net put down.

"In one good season a fish station used to take $3700 in salmon." And that in a time when salmon was 5 cents to 10 cents a pound.

She remembered the name of every rock that meant a foothold for an Indian fisherman in the brawling torrent; sites now drowned by the lake back of The Dalles dam.

(continued)

Chinook rock … Standing rock … Big Island.

Big Island was the largest, driest rock outcropping in the Celilo formation, at the western end. Part of it lay under the railroad bridge. During the season when the fish were coming upriver in flotillas, Wy-ams camped on Big Island to make the work of harvesting salmon a little easier.

Access to this rock island was by the bridge. Flora remarked that she had often watched with fear as Indian mothers climbed the rope ladder with a papoose tied to their backs.

Mrs. Thompson told a touching story of the time a small fire in her home charred "our national colors," as she calls the American flag used by the Wy-ams during their festival of the salmon.

The Wasco county sheriff viewed the ruined flag and mumbled his sympathy. Flora was deeply saddened by the loss. "I treasured my national colors."

Some time later a package came to her from Washington, D.C. In it lay a beautiful, big American flag, along with a letter explaining that it had flown over the Capitol when Dwight Eisenhower was President.

The letter continued, because Flora and her people felt the loss of their "national colors" so deeply, the writer thought that this particular flag should belong to the Wy-ams. It was signed "Al Ullman, Representative."

With obvious relish Mrs. Thompson told this story:

It was the first time she and the chief, his daughter and son-in-law attended a Wasco Pioneer Association dinner in The Dalles, long ago.

In their handsomest native dress they stood in line to register. They received the usual nametags and Flora, first in line, was asked if they were members of the Pioneer organization.

Flora was silent. Chief Tommy whispered to her in their native tongue. "Why don't you tell them who we are?"

You could imagine the little Indian woman drawing her five-foot frame to its most regal height as she faced the questioner and answered, "Don't think I'm insulting you. You want to know the truth. I'll tell you. We were here to receive the pioneers!"

She smiles with satisfaction as she tells that one.

A young Parkdaler asked the chief's widow if she would dance to the Indian music being played on a record. Flora shook her head.

"You don't dance to that," she said saucily. "You smoke a pipe."

But she did sing an Indian gospel hymn. A "traditional" gospel hymn, she amended.

The drum she used to accompany herself had been given her by Alice and Charley Slimjim of Hood River. It was a round cylinder over which a piece of rawhide was stretched. She held it by the taut double thongs on the back, using a flannel-covered drumstick she had made for Chief Tommy.

As Flora sang the minor melody in her native tongue, her eyes closed, the slow cadence of the drum became a hypnotic background for the crooning voice singing of "the echo of the drum that sends the spirit along the road like an eagle flying."

To the hushed listeners it was a slice of history brought alive in Parkdale, the voice of a people from long ago, sadly watching the old ways go, but confident of eternal salvation if their spirit took the right road like an eagle flying.

On Monday little Mrs. Thompson visited Parkdale Elementary school. And you may wager an eagle feather that the students will be telling their children and grandchildren about that visit some day.

Oct. 11, 1973

— ☙ —

Tom McCall

Governor Tom McCall slept there as a small boy. So did his mother, Dorothy Lawson McCall, and his father, Hal McCall. And his grandfather, financier Thomas Lawson of Boston. So did many famous and near-famous.

The Cottage Farm summer resort on Belmont road, now the Hood River Care Center, was without a doubt the most popular refuge for tired, wealthy vacationers in the whole state of Oregon.

It was the only place of its kind within commuting distance of Portland from the time it opened in 1894 until well into the 1900s — a quiet, pastoral summering place with excellent food and the gentlewomanly ministrations of its owner, Mrs. Alma Howe, who was a genteel hostess and a practical nurse.

The guest book read like a list of Portland's Four Hundred: Kerrs ... Corbetts ... Ladds ... Teals ... Lawrences ... and millionaire Thomas W. Lawson of Boston, grandfather of Governor McCall.

Hal and Dorothy McCall first came to the Cottage Farm in March 1911. They returned in June with copper king Lawson. He was then looking for a farm for his son-in-law, newly arrived in Portland from Boston. McCall had been told to get out in the wide open spaces for the sake of his health.

Lawson looked over Hood River Valley, loved it, adored Mrs. Howe and her cooking at the Cottage Farm. The resort by then had one main building, recently enlarged, with 33 guest rooms, a large dining room and several tents.

Alma Howe then owned 11 acres, from which much of the food came. Later, several comfortable cottages for guests were added.

The McCalls settled near Prineville but Thomas Lawson returned to the Cottage Farm many times during his trips west. He was charmed by Mrs. Howe, a highly intelligent, forthright woman. He admired her compassion for the Indians and her knowledge of their ways.

During her 48 years in Hood River at the same place on Belmont road, Mrs. Howe did more to ease the sad plight of local Indians than any other person. She was their counselor, friend, nurse, financier, lawyer.

She fought for their rights; she looked after men in their old age; she gave some a home.

When the McCall children were old enough, Lawson often brought them to stay at Mrs. Howe's, accompanied by a nurse for the younger ones.

There are people today who remember attending Miss Kitty Bragg's dancing class in town where a tall, thin boy with a strange accent occasionally popped up. It was Tom McCall.

One dancer will never forget him. She claims that she dreaded having him as a partner because he always clung to the long garters which, in those days, were attached to a belt at the waist to hold a girl's stockings up.

It is preferable to think that the future governor unconsciously grabbed his partner's garter in his boyish nervousness. The lady still claims that he did it on purpose.

Thomas Lawson died in Boston in 1925. By then the day of the summer resort had passed. In 1931 Mrs. Howe sold the Cottage Farm and went to live in the Salem Methodist home at the age of 71.

1974, Panorama, Hood River News

— ⊗ —

Edna Loving

Nominated for Gardener of the Year 1976 — Edna Loving. You passed her "farm" downtown last summer and didn't know it.

Edna has an apartment over the Paris Fair annex. She transformed a miserable rocky plot out back into a beautiful little

(continued)

garden and flower bed, even a stand of corn. On the veranda overlooking Oak Street, tomato plants to the ceiling, begonias blooming into November, a lush jungle.

Jan. 13, 1977

— ❧ —

ABE LINCOLN

The Honorable Ezra Smith, dean of local "horticulturalists" in the old days, saw Abraham Lincoln at the 1860 Republican convention. He told the HR Glacier in 1912:

"I thought that Abe Lincoln was the homeliest man I had ever seen … He had extraordinarily long legs and was ungainly about the waist but he lost his homeliness when he began to talk. I never heard a more magnetic voice."

Lincoln aficionados, among them attorney Ken Abraham, may have heard the story, probably fictitious, which the Hon. [Ezra] Smith told:

> Lincoln was walking in the woods one day and met another man who raised a gun as if to shoot him. When asked why, the man replied that he had determined, if he ever met an uglier man than himself, he would kill him.

> Cried Lincoln, "For God's sake shoot, if I am any homelier than you.

Feb. 10, 1977

— ❧ —

BRUCE JENNER

The lean young man looked faintly familiar to me as he wandered around the book department of a Portland store. Oh yes — Wheaties commercials.

It was Bruce Jenner, the decathlon star of the Montreal Olympics, waiting for wife Chrystie to finish autographing her first book. How fleeting TV fame, when you are only recognized from a current ad for cereal. P.S. He's beautiful but his strength isn't in his hair, which is thinning.

Oct. 27, 1977

— ❧ —

THE SU FAMILY

A highlight of 1979 was the arrival of a son to Grace and Kok Djen Su, proprietors of the Sundown Restaurant.

Now nearly four months old, the little boy is called Mei Shen, which means "Beautiful Life," but his full name is Justin Alexander Mei Shen.

The young Su couple came to Hood River from Indonesia Java by way of Seattle, where they met while in college. The reason they specialize in North China dishes at the Sundown: Because their families came originally from there.

Jan. 3, 1980

— ❧ —

KATHLEEN NICHOLS

Our bronze medal with appleleaf clusters for the whole past winter season must go to Kathleen (Mrs. Dick) Nichols, chairman of the Hood River County Museum Board.

Many times through those cold months while the Museum was officially closed Kathleen opened, warmed and dusted it up for visits from Portland travel clubs. These groups of older people came by bus, usually about 40 strong. One busload arrived the day before Christmas. They are still coming.

The visit of an hour pleases and surprises most of the club members, who come from various points around Portland. They

(continued)

don't expect to find such an attractive and orderly museum in a little town like Hood River.

Kathleen tops off the hour with renditions of old-timey numbers on the 1909 player piano, a gift from Juanita Glaze Schroeder. It's a tossup who enjoys the music most, Kathleen or the visitors, who board their bus with smiles and the glint of happily remembered times past.

May 8, 1980

— ❧ —

Roy Webster

"It could have been embarrassing if he hadn't been so gallant," she said.

Inez Young Lamer, who grew up in Hood River, attends an aquatic class at the MAC pool in Portland. During one session she noticed a distinguished-looking swimmer with resistors on both arms as he plowed through the water.

Upon inquiry, he said he was getting in shape for senior swim competition. Inez suggested that he ought to get in touch "with a little old man in Hood River who swims the Columbia every Labor Day."

Whereupon, 83-year-old Roy Webster stood up to his considerable height in the pool and announced, "I AM that little old man!"

June 6, 1984

— ❧ —

CHAPTER 5

SIGNS OF THE TIMES

*— A wise woman comments on
society and politics*

ELECTRONIC MULTI-TASKER

There's a man-after-me-own-heart near here. Has his alarm clock rigged up so that when it chirps happily in the a.m. it turns on the radio and starts the automatic coffeemaker. When he perfects the mechanism to put up lunches and cook the oatmeal, I'll buy it!

Sept. 18, 1951, Hood River Daily Sun

— ℭℜ —

SUPPORT THE LIBRARY

The local library situation growing out of a recent decision by the attorney general is a worrier. To the surprise of all, including the city, the A-G ruled that it is a county library. The city is no longer legally obliged to help support it.

When the city council and county court meet tonight, all of us interested in maintaining the library at its present high level — it does have a splendid record among Oregon libraries — [should show up.] Hope the members will consider that city taxpayers have a moral if not a legal obligation to fulfill. We unquestioningly pay taxes for schools, and certainly the library is a necessary part of the community's educational program. It is vital not only to schoolchildren, but to all of us adults who would be lost without it.

March 10, 1952, Hood River Daily Sun

— ℭℜ —

THE KINDERGARTEN DEBATE

Being able to state both sides of a public problem is one of the nice things about the United States. Casting about for the opinions on the HR kindergarten question, have so far heard only one side:

Mrs. A, a graduate in education, specializing in kindergarten, who has pre-schoolers … I'm going to vote against having

(continued)

kindergarten in the school system at this time. Any money available should be spent on more important projects, There is a need for remedial work, for example, and a teacher with 27 pupils hasn't time for five among them who need help.

Mrs. B ... Pre-schoolers' problems should be solved at home. But our schoolchildren need more individual attention if we are going to cope with juvenile delinquency. Let's have more teachers, better school facilities and more time for cooperation between parents and teachers.

Mrs. C ... Is kindergarten such a crying need? I don't feel like paying taxes for babysitters. It's pretty well established that most children don't need and aren't ready for group work until they are six!

Anyone on the other side have an argument? Let's hear from you. Names not necessary.

April 7, 1952, Hood River Daily Sun

— ℭℜ —

EFFICIENCY ON THE HIGHWAYS

First, you meet a state truck from which a large paper sack, assorted pieces of paper and other debris are being tossed as it travels towards Portland. Two miles later you meet a state truck parked, with men picking up paper sacks, assorted pieces of paper and other debris.

April 15, 1955

— ℭℜ —

TV MANNERS

Someone's TV manners are showing! Business woman was justifiably irate one Sunday. Received an anonymous phone demand that she turn off her washing machine so the caller could get a program more clearly. Solution — ask the TV neighbor to do your washing for you during the week!

June 24, 1955

— ∝ —

Does time rule?

Said the Queen in "Alice in Wonderland": He's murdering the time; off with his head!"

These days the tables are turned. Time is the master! Several White Salmon women took in the Washington PTA convention in Spokane and came home most impressed with a psych professor Jones. He told them that, of the three major fears today — the atom bomb, time and economic pressures — time is the greatest.

The clock, says Prof. Jones, masters us, dominates both our conscious and unconscious life. This subservience we pass on to our children.

We suggest an interesting experiment: Before school begins, arrange a day when no one in the family looks at the clock from morning 'til night. We dare you! Needless to say, it will take a good deal of calendar and clock-watching to arrange the day!

Aug. 19, 1955

— ∝ —

New medium critique, part 1

Although television is a wonderful medium of entertainment, this quiet voice of wisdom speaks in the wilderness. It is Dr. Frank Baxter, an eminent TV performer himself, who decries the reading of good books among youngsters.

(continued)

Says Dr. Baxter:

> The alarming thing today is not the use but the abuse of television. Parents rely on it as a sort of opiate to keep their children quiet and out of circulation. Unfortunately, television encourages passivity rather than activity. It is easy. It is habit-forming. It fosters the dangerous idea that we can learn by letting knowledge drip on us like rain from heaven … Only the written word gives students the solid background that underlies all real culture.
>
> *Sept. 23, 1955*

— CR —

LOCAL PRIDE

Used to be you could scare off door-to-door salesmen with a truthful statement about lack of money. But no more! Nowadays that is merely a come-on for their credit pitch.

There is, however, one answer guaranteed to turneth away the most persistent out-of-town salesmen. "No," you say firmly, "we earn our living in this community, and when we buy, we'll buy at home!" It works.

Oct. 7, 1955

— CR —

WHERE'S THE LOGIC?

Aunt Illi says, "I just don't figure today's economics, like when so many mothers have to take jobs to buy time-saving appliances so they can work!"

To which we add that there must be something screwy in the present-day setup whereby parents are so busy going to organizational meetings for their children's organizations that they have little time to spend at home with those same children!

Jan. 26, 1956

— ∞ —

HEROINE, 1956

Cast a bronze medal and lift the latch
For the gal who still makes her cake from scratch!

— ∞ —

NEW FOR 1958 …

electrical brain construction kit, called Geniac. "Solves problems faster than you can express them." Priced at $19.95 … Unitron for watching satellites go by, $125 and up … Star Pointer picks out any constellation or individual stars, $4.95.

Jan. 2, 1958

— ∞ —

SPUTNIK GAZING

A number of local early birds saw Sputnik III tumble across the morning sky June 18, right on schedule. Next morning it was due at 3:40 and a lot of us were running around the lawns in nighties and pajamas, but no Sputnik, so far as we could see. This may be psychological warfare at its grimmest … keeping the whole country on tippy-toe in the night to see Sputnik appear, then changing its course so that it deviates to another section unexpectedly, until the population is frazzle-nerved and sleepless and an easy prey to conquest!

June 26, 1958

— ∞ —

New medium critique, part 2

TV can be downright dangerous! Philadelphia doctor advises viewers to get up and walk around at least once an hour to avoid risk of getting serious leg disorders.

He reports three cases of dangerous blood clots in leg vessels of patients who had been sitting in awkward positions watching TV. One man sat with back of knees pressed against the edge of the chair for an hour and a half, another with his leg thrown over the arm of a chair and a woman with her leg tucked under. So beware!

Sept. 18, 1958

— & —

Disaster aid

Ironic, indeed, that the group selling Washington firecrackers to Oregon youngsters for illegal use was the White Salmon fire dept. With the funds to go toward a disaster truck!

July 9, 1959

— & —

Opinions welcome

Local headlines would give the impression that every soul in HR is endlessly embroiled in bitter controversy over schools, community development, roads, electricity, city and county business. This is merely America in action. Better we should have expressions of opposition than no opinions at all. The time for Hood River to worry will be when no one objects to anything!

July 16, 1959

— & —

PROBLEMS SOLVED

What are we worrying about? No matter which man wins the presidency, we are going to have better schools … higher incomes … a mightier nation … a government which will solve all the world's problems in short order … more housing … more help in our old age … greater humanity to men of all colors … solution of the farm problem with everyone happy about it … peace … a crash program into space.

And it's not going to cost us a cent more. They said so.

Nov. 3, 1960

— ❧ —

A NOBLE OCCUPATION

See in the Sunday papers some opinions on use of the term "housewife," which is a coincidence, because a Hood River mother was just telling us an experience she had recently.

She was stopped by a local policeman for some minor traffic violation. It was not being stopped that burned her. It was what the young man said, quote, "Do you have an occupation or are you just a housewife?"

Well, sir, it's like this sir. This young woman's occupation (that which engages one's time and attention — Webster) IS as "housewife," and not "just a"! She has three small children and a husband to attend, she manages a charming home, is an expert landscaper and gardener, seamstress, artist, entertains delightfully and often can plan and buy food for 100 people for a month, works like a trooper on community drives, teaches Red Cross swimming, tends her husband's hunting dogs, skillfully executes any job she is given.

Yes sir, she's a "housewife" with all the dignity inherent in that term, and if that isn't an "occupation" we'll treat you to tea.

Dec. 8, 1960

— ❧ —

Is a strike next?

Rumor has it that we're in Dutch with a good many husbands, after quoting figures last week on a young mother's worth to her family. Seems the gals want their allowances raised!

Dec. 15, 1960

— ∞ —

Selling Easter

Having labored in the happy vineyards of Portland's big store writing advertising copy at one time, we avidly read the fruits of Meier & Frank copywriters.

Prize copy appeared recently … about Easter being just a hippity hop away and the children all needing new Easter outfits and how you, with your happy habit of shopping at M&F … frequently … can take advantage of their wise and comfortable family-planned credit "to make your Easter shopping spree free of pain or budget strain."

Punch line — "All it takes is a Charga-Plate for a happy Easter at M&F"! This ought to make an excellent title for some reverend gentleman's Easter sermon.

March 23, 1961

— ∞ —

Khrushchev's vision

The following comment should stand in 14-point bold face print at the head of every newspaper and magazine page, should be permanently embroidered in every American mind as we read what's going on in our country.

It is a little-noticed statement by Nikita Khrushchev, who said it three and a half months before his last visit to the U.S.:

We cannot expect Americans to jump from capitalism to communism, but we can assist their elected leaders in giving Americans small doses of socialism, until they suddenly awake to find they have communism.

Dec. 14, 1961

— ❧ —

"Silent Spring" Review

"Be sure to read Rachel Carson's article in the June 16th New Yorker," caller said. "It will scare the wits out of you!" only he used stronger language.

He was so right. The magazine thought "Silent Spring" by respected scientist Carson important enough to let it run continuously from page 35 to page 99 in the issue. It is only the first of three articles.

The disarming title little prepares you for the subject — the corruption of and irrevocable damage to man's environment by his own hand through use of insecticides or "Biocides," as the author calls them, on plants and food, in soil, rivers, air.

Everyone should read this article. We hope it will be condensed in the Reader's Digest.

Every orchardist, every gardener, every handler of insecticides should know the abnormal nature of the 500 new manmade chemicals "to which the bodies of men and all other living things are required somehow to adapt each year — chemicals totally outside the biological experience."

Those who cannot or will not face realities won't read the Carson article. Those with a sense of obligation to and concern for the future of the human race will be troubled by it as they go about their spraying of trees, gardens, roadsides, lakes, animals. But it will help to know just what we are dealing with.

(continued)

Says Miss Carson, who wrote the best-selling "The Sea Around Us," "If we are going to live so intimately with these chemicals — eating and drinking them, taking them into the very marrow of our bones — we had better know something about their power."

The author is concerned with the new man-made insecticides produced by manipulation of molecules, because they differ sharply from the prewar poisonous chemicals derived from naturally occurring minerals and plant products.

Danger in the synthetic insecticides is their tremendous biological potency, whose results can only be guessed at now. As Miss Carson writes, "They can enter into the most vital processes of the body and change them in sinister and often deadly ways."

It is impossible to condense such an article properly. A few main points must suffice:

> The majority of modern insecticides fall into one of two large groups of chemicals:
>
> 1. Chlorinated hydrocarbons, represented by DDT.
>
> 2. Organic phosphates such as malathion and parathion.
>
> It is not widely understood that, upon entering the body, the storage of many of these chemicals is in fatty depots such as the adrenals, testes, thyroid, and even in larger storage depositories like the liver, kidney and fat of the tissue that enfolds the intestines.
>
> Although the intake may be the smallest conceivable amount, these storage depots act as biological magnifiers and bring about a hundredfold increase as they pile up within the body, causing alarming changes in the human organism. Harmful effects may not occur for years.
>
> DDT and related chemicals are passed on from one organism to another — alfalfa to meal to hen or egg to human. Or alfalfa to hay to cow to milk to human.

The concentration increases wildly as it passes through fatty substances.

Chlordane has DDT's evils, plus a few of its own. Its residue persists in soil, on foodstuffs and on surfaces sprayed. It takes advantage of all available entries to the body.

A diet including 2.5 parts per million of chlordane may lead in time to storage of 75 parts per million in the fat.

A Food and Drug Administration official has described it as "one of the most toxic of insecticides. Anyone handling it could be poisoned."

In the 1930s, the chlorinated naphthalenes, a special group to which dieldrin, aldrin and endrin belong, were found to be causing hepatitis and a fatal disease known as yellow atrophy of the liver.

These chemicals have led to illness and death of workers in electrical industries where they were used in insulation. They are also thought to be a cause of a mysterious and usually fatal disease in cows.

Dieldrin, aldrin and endrin are among the most violently poisonous of all.

Dieldrin is about five times as toxic as DDT when it enters the body through the mouth, and 40 times as toxic absorbed through the skin in solution. It is believed to lie dormant in the human body, to flare up in periods of physiological stress, when the body draws upon its fat reserves.

Aldrin has produced degenerative changes in the liver and kidneys of experimental animals. A quantity the size of an asprin tablet is enough to kill more than 400 quail. Small amounts also cause sterility in animals under study.

(continued)

Endrin is 12 times as poisonous to rats as dieldrin. It has killed vast numbers of fish as well as cattle wandering into sprayed orchards and has poisoned wells.

A case is cited in which an American couple went to live in Venezuela in 1958. A spray containing endrin was used to kill cockroaches in the houses, followed by washing of the floors.

The baby and family dog were brought back some six hours later. The dog died within an hour. The baby is alive, but little more than a vegetable, with little hope of improvement.

The organic-phosphates, including malathion and parathion, destroy enzymes in the living body. It is considered important, states Miss Carson, that spray operators and others regularly exposed have periodic examination of the blood.

This is only the start of a chilling series of articles. Unlike some alarmists, worried scientists believe they have an alternative to indiscriminate spraying — biological controls and selective spraying.

After reading the first installment we wonder, hearing of an orchardist who spends a good deal of his spraying time humanely covering occupied bird nests with his hat — we wonder if he has given as much thought to his own and his family's protection against the poison he is using.

From idle curiosity we have just read the label on a seemingly innocent soil dust sitting carelessly around the house. We had applied it earlier with gay abandon to the garden, even to some edible plants.

Contents: DDT, 20 per cent … chlordane, 5 per cent … adrin, 5 per cent.

Now we note in small print at the bottom, "Do not apply this product to soils in which edible root crops will be planted."

Also, "Do not apply or allow to drift to areas occupied by unprotected humans or beneficial animals."

Yet it is recommended for coverage of lawns!

July 5, 1962

— ⍟ —

SPRAY DAMAGE

This spray problem is not a mere figment of Rachel Carson's imagination, although she may have over-dramatized it in her book, "Silent Spring." No matter how much some groups have wanted to play it down, the lid is being pried off Pandora's box.

A consulting forester in Portland said to us, "There is going to be legislation eventually. We know we are doing damage in the forests when we spray. Yet many foresters hate to admit it or to face the problem. It's easier to keep our eyes on the spruce budworm than to get involved in this whole complex thing."

Nov. 1, 1962

— ⍟ —

THE RACHEL CARSON DEBATE

In all these years, the topic bringing this column the most vehement response was the review last summer of Rachel Carson's book on sprays, "Silent Spring."

It has provoked a steady flow of material, mostly con, a visit from a businessman from the city very pro-Carson, and several lectures to us by local orchardists and spray representatives.

Via the grapevine, we understand that a prominent Portland TV commentator planned a half-hour show on the spray problem in

(continued)

Oregon last October. Because of pressures, his original outline for the show was so watered-down that he despaired of doing a factually honest report. If he ever put on the program at all, we didn't hear about it.

March 28, 1963

— ❧ —

ENEMY EDUCATION

Authorities want public reaction to a proposal that Oregon schools teach students about communism. Some people, without thinking this one through, are writing horrified letters to editors.

A noted educator had the best answer. Receiving a protest to courses about communism in his university, he asked if medical colleges should stop teaching about cancer.

How can we fight without knowing the nature of the thing against which we must fight?

April 19, 1964

— ❧ —

THE SORT OF THING THAT MAKES WOMEN WANT TO LEAVE HOME —

recent newspaper reference to "housewives and other unskilled workers." Technically correct and maybe all too true, such classification is no help to the little woman's self-esteem.

May 28, 1964

— ❧ —

ASSASSINATION POSTSCRIPT

The Arlo Ordways, home in Hobbs, New Mexico after their Hood River visit in November, felt the impact of President Kennedy's murder on the southwest. Their camera slides, apparently processed in Dallas, came back with a white slip, printed in red.

It said: "PRESIDENTS ASSASSINATION — Should this film contain pictures taken of President Kennedy's assassination, call your local FBI office immediately."

Jan. 9, 1964

— ∝ —

TV CAN BE TRAUMATIC ...

for small children, as the Ericksons discovered. Spence has been taking part in a TV program on Social Security. He also referees televised basketball games. When son David, age three, first saw his dad on the screen, he searched behind the set, crawled underneath, emerged and looked at Spence quizzically. "Daddy," he asked, "are you two people?"

Sept. 23, 1965

— ∝ —

FUEL EFFICIENCY, CIRCA 1915

In a 1915 HR News, it was reported that E.L. McClain, then owner of Van Horn butte, had received by boat from Portland a brand new Franklin automobile.

A test run of this car in the city had produced a gas mileage of 43.8 miles per gallon, and the Franklin was a heavy auto. This was not up to the U.S. champion of 1914, however. In a test run that year, the winner got 51.2 and the average for all 94 cars was 32.8 There was no reference to speed.

Feb. 25, 1966

— ∝ —

Applause and Tears

That announcement by the Wy-east graduating class that their school "gift" of around $400 was to go to a hospital in South Viet Nam got to the commencement audience. Applause erupted, was prolonged and drowned out the sound of tears splashing from adult eyes. There was some nose-blowing.

Principal Chuck Bowe says he understood that the class vote on the very original and very humanitarian ideas was "overwhelming."

To the 1966 graduating class of Wy-east High school, our bronze medal with apple leaf clusters for June.

June 9, 1966

— ℞ —

View on a Clear Day

More on air pollution. Friends of ours, the Paulen Kasebergs, perched a mobile trailer on a high point at the edge of their Sherman county wheat lands this year. They were trying out the view before deciding whether to build a home there.

On a clear day from their living room they look down into the chasm of the Deschutes river, thousands of feet below. Westward, they see The Dalles area with a glint of the Columbia river at Crates Point. The snowcapped backbone of the Cascade range forms their southern and northern horizon. On a clear night, they see the glow of Portland lights behind Mount Defiance's silhouette.

But how many clear days and nights this year? Very few! The canyons and valleys from the Columbia south have been everlastingly filled with blue-gray haze. The Kasebergs figure this split pea soup has to be car exhausts, some of The Dalles' industrial smoke and maybe even Portland's.

Then along came the new power transmission lines, very close, cutting across their view to the north. So there's no escaping progress and its accompanying pollution, even in the wide spaces of Sherman county.

Oct. 5, 1967

— ∞ —

FOOD FOR YOUNG THOUGHT

Editha Hartwig Keppel, affectionately remembered here, writes from Berkeley, Cal., where she teaches in the big high school.

Commenting on the social problems as she sees them there, she adds, "I'm glad I grew up in Hood River." She sent along a talk given by a former teacher, Dan Moore, now educational director for the LA Times. His ideas of what bugs the youngsters of today present a picture which is food for thought.

1. Half of the U.S. population is under 25 for the first time in our or any nation's history. In a few years they will be an absolute voting majority "and they will be able to vote in or vote out anything they want to — including us."

2. We have been teaching them to question, to reason, to attack our logic and not to accept everything they read. Now we are shocked because they are doing those things.

3. They are different because they are the first of a whole new world shaping up in one generation. We older ones are the last generation of a way of life.

For instance, you can't starve to death in civilized America any more. They won't let you; they'll force-feed you the rest of your life, if need be. Dad used to say he worked to keep from starving to death.

(continued)

The young generation knows this isn't true today. So, is work necessary, they ask?

They may not even have to work. A Presidential commission has proposed that one answer to automation is for every one to retire at 38. The 20-hour week is right around the corner. In not too many years, at the rate automation is increasing, two percent of the population will be able to produce all the goods and services necessary to take care of all the rest.

Dec. 7, 1967

— ∞ —

DROWNING THE PAST

Many traveled east to watch the "miracle" of monstrous Umatilla Lake growing behind John Day Dam. At the same time it was creating future power and recreation for men, it was sadly drowning a human past in the petroglyphs now under water, and destroying the sanctuary of birds and small animals. Some argue that the water is still there for waterfowl and birds which nest close to water. Yes, but the protective covering is gone. If you have ever seen a crow snatch naked chicks from their nest, you know that no bird can raise its brood along the river unless it is well hidden. Now there is no place to hide and the breeding birds will not come next spring.

May 9, 1968

— ∞ —

DISAPPEARING NEWS

Newspaper people shiver with apprehension. It is ego-deflating enough to know that, shortly after publication, the words they struggle over end up wrapped around garbage or in the bottom of bird cages.

Pity the poor writer now. A new paper has been developed which disintegrates when dropped into water! Dissolves, disappears completely, non-toxic, odorless.

June 27, 1968

—❧—

SMART STING OF THE SWITCH

Aunt Illi was raised in a pre-Spockian epoch when youngsters got punished every time they richly deserved it. The most flagrant violations resulted in a good, smart sting with a poplar switch. She didn't hate her parents, either.

Now Aunt Illi says, "I've got a solution for this trouble in the colleges. The administration should announce that if there is any violence at all, the college will be closed indefinitely to everyone. The 98 per cent of the student body not throwing tantrums would take care of the two per cent which is! And the small segment of professors teaching violent protest would be attended to by the rest of the faculty. And that would be that."

Nov. 28, 1968

—❧—

TOGETHER, EVERYBODY

First exercise of the New year: Write fifty times by hand, "1969 … 1969 … 1969," etc.

Those snatches of the Apollo 8 trip viewed on TV, exciting as they were, couldn't compare with the experience of people living in the islands.

Mary Campbell Hedell wrote from Kealakekua, Island of Hawaii, on Saturday morning Dec. 21:

> … we saw Apollo 8 go through the skies this morning right on schedule, 5:45 a.m., from west

(continued)

to east, and we also saw the thrust, or "burst" that sends it to the moon!

First of all, we set the alarm for 2:30 a.m. and watched via Lani Bird the Apollo 8 blast off, then set the alarm again for 5:30 a.m. and went into our yard to the south. We've had a week of rainy weather, our usual winter storm, but the skies cleared last evening as though to make it possible for us to view that spectacle. Sure enough, right on schedule it came through the sky. It was dark, of course, at that hour, the sky filled with brilliant stars, no moon, so … we saw this tremendous thrust which lit up the sky. After that, on it went to the moon!

Jan 2, 1969

— ℭℜ —

Rootless families

Predictions are that Oregon will see more unemployed men, more dislocated and rootless families arriving in the state this year than ever before. Figures show that they are already coming in large numbers, mainly from California and Washington.

Who are they, why are they coming to Oregon, what is their outlook for the future? Here's the story of two young families which, while probably not typical, is at least symptomatic of the times.

Paid til Easter

Two young men, slightly bearded but clean, arrived in Hood River with backpacks early in April. They had left their wives and three young children in southern California while they hiked north.

Their first concern was a place to live so that their families could join them. Between them, the two had $70. They frankly told a motel owner so. Making a quick and shrewd appraisal of the two, he rented them one large motel unit, paid up to Easter Sunday.

Somehow, the families got here, with very few possessions. Two young wives and three toddlers. Clean, attractive and glad to be with the men.

Who were they and why had they come to Hood River? Well, they'd worked in the fruit before, they thought they could hunt and fish for food when necessary, and they love the forests and mountains.

The one we'll call John is 28. He was born in Indiana, but grew up on a farm east of Gresham.

When a boy

"I loved it there when I was a boy. Beautiful country, rolling farms. Now it makes me sick to my stomach. No farms, just houses. They aren't even working that good land."

He has brothers who are professional men. "I just sort of wandered around after I finished high school."

He drifted into carpenter work, welding. An accident in which his small pickup was rear-ended broke his back in three places and ended his ability to do heavy work. He and his wife have two small children.

A will to stay

The younger man – we'll call him Bob – was born in Tacoma. A high school graduate, he has no skill. He has done farm work in this area off and on. He and his wife have one child.

Both men say they've learned their lesson, by their own mistakes and that of others. They hate to see their families suffer. "The Lord blessed us both with good wives. They never complain."

They added, "If we hadn't bounced around all these years we wouldn't be in this fix. What we've got to do is put down roots, find places where our families can stay put. If we could just find a couple of little old houses that we could fix up ..."

(continued)

Place to live

Even though they talked most about security in terms of a place to live, work was very much on their minds, too.

"We'll work at anything. We don't want handouts or welfare if we can help it. We've seen what it does to people. We had this friend who was able-bodied but he got to depending on that welfare check and he decided it's easier to sit back and let it come. He's turned into a bum."

They acknowledge their work limitations. To them it seems too late to get specialized training, although they spoke vaguely of taking some vocational courses.

Brothers help

These two families, rootless, unskilled and impoverished, represent a growing religious movement among some of the young. There have been times, they maintain, when their faith in God was the only thing that kept them going.

They think of themselves as evangelists. They feel that they are living according to the Word, and they try to pass it along to other young people. Their faith is contagious.

"We've been trying to carry the Lord's word wherever we go. We feel He'll see us through. He has in the past."

Wherever they settle, they find "brothers" with whom they form a small group in fellowship. They are familiar through study with every Bible translation, but they prefer the beauty and inspiration of the King James version.

Food abundant

Through the operation of the FISH project in Hood River, the two young men were informed that they could get supplies from the Abundant Foods program in The Dalles. Grateful for transportation to the store, the two were overwhelmed with the stock of food they received.

"We haven't seen this much food in months! Wait 'til our wives see all this." Rice, spaghetti, flour, sugar, canned juice and vegetables, prunes, canned meat, other items.

In The Dalles store they were remembered because of a newspaper story about them last fall. The men didn't know they made headlines because they had taken their families to California following the happening.

Snow-cat saviors

During harvest season last year they cleared $400. Thinking to save it for a leaner winter, the two families took John's old station wagon into the Camp Baldwin area. They planned to camp for a while, fish and hunt to save money on food and rent.

They had scarcely settled in when an early snow hit. It fell not in inches, but in feet. The car was immovable and they were marooned in the deep snow, poorly prepared for winter.

Fire-spotter planes flew over but no one saw their signals for help. They found a roof of sorts where they could keep the children warm.

For one month the adults ate sparingly, read their Bibles, and prayed for help. They never really got to the point where they gave up hope.

Help came in numbers. Men riding nine snow-cats brought into the area for a demonstration happened on the young families. "Praise the Lord!" Bob and John still exclaim as they tell of their rescue.

The station wagon is still up there, buried in snow.

Unwavering faith

There is a sequel to the story, but not an ending.

Through the local employment office, John and Bob found short-term work on a valley farm. Best of all, the owner let them over their families into a fair-sized cabin in exchange for work. "Our prayers have been answered again!"

(continued)

The two men had absolute and unwavering faith that things were going to be all right, that they would find work somewhere to tide the five of them over until harvest season.

Easter Sunday no longer became a deadline. They had a place for their families. In celebration of their good fortune, one of the fellows gave his wife an Easter gift: a pair of knitting needles she had been wanting.

All of those who came in contact with them have less hope for the future of these people than they themselves. And more than one person must have thought of them on Easter Day, and worried a little about what next month and next year hold for them, the rootless, the unskilled.

April 15, 1971

— ⚮ —

MOTHERS' WORTH

In case you women missed a small news item during the summer: A federal appeals court upheld a Cincinnati jury's decision that the work of a mother of nine children was worth 2.50 an hour. This thinking was the basis for an amount awarded the family of a woman killed in an auto accident.

The decision was based on statistics from the Ohio Bureau of Employment service showing that it would cost at least 2.50 an hour to have an outsider do the dead mother's work. So now you mommies can take an hour for fun stuff without feeling guilty. After all, it was only worth 2.50!

Sept. 6, 1973

— ⚮ —

THE CRONKITE DIET ...

introduced some time back is still effective for year-end flab. You have your dinner in front of the TV set when Walter is on and you eat only if there's good news. It works just as well with John and David or Barbara and Harry.

Jan. 13, 1977

— CR —

LISTEN UP, MEN

Any man with designs on the presidency in four or eight years had better start planning right now how to top the Carters' 16-block walk down Pennsylvania avenue last Thursday. A masterly public relations move.

And husbands should get used to holding hands with their wives in public. "Jimmy Carter does it so why can't you?"

Jan. 27, 1977

— CR —

FOR HOMEMAKERS ONLY

Show this to your husband at your own risk.

A current best seller, "Passages," footnotes an estimate of a housewife's economic value in 1974 made by the Washington Post and based on interviews with mothers of two children.

Pricing on the open market, the same service they performed, the total came to $793.60 a week. Today, three years later, it would be much higher.

In 25 years of in-home service, the total would be a contribution of $1,124,500. Yet, as the author points out, a woman cannot collect unemployment insurance for losing her job as a wife nor, when she becomes a widow, is she considered to have contributed to her husband's estate, which is taxed at the highest rate.

Oct. 13, 1977

— CR —

An early example of discrimination

City ordinance no. 110 passed by the Common Council in 1906 forbade the selling or giving of "any spirituous, vinous or malt liquors" to any minor, any woman, any Indian. The penalty was stiff.

It also prohibited "any minor or woman to frequent, visit or loiter" in a drinking shop or tipping house.

Oct. 27, 1977

— ℞ —

Women have made one small step ...

towards more personal identity. The new telephone directory shows many more wives listed by their given names. That's good.

Less apparent but occasionally noted these days in newspapers is the inclusion of a woman's maiden surname in her obituary. The implication in death notices has been that a woman had no identity until wed. Or that, at the point of marriage, her former identity was erased.

Including the maiden name in an obituary restores the sense of a whole life and is a reminder that a wife had "roots" of her own.

June 14, 1979

— ℞ —

It takes a dedicated jogger ...

to sense environmental changes sooner than the rest of us.

Bob Lausmann, a faithful jogger, notices increasing pollution of Hood River's formerly unsullied air. There is a smoke pall over his jogging route, and a smell which has to be from wood burning, he says.

Jan. 3, 1980

— ℞ —

WHAT TALES WE'LL HAVE FOR OUR GRANDCHILDREN!

"I remember when I used to run the hot water faucet in the kitchen sink to make steam for my African violets."

"We set the thermostat at 72 all day, lowered it to 68 nighttimes."

"When I needed something I didn't have for a special recipe, I jumped in the car and drove to the grocery."

"Never even used to know how much heating oil we used each year. It wasn't that big a deal."

"It only cost fifteen cents to send a letter."

Feb. 14, 1980

—〇З—

IF PORTLAND'S GARBAGE BY TRUCK ...

turns the Columbia Gorge into a Veil of Offal in the near future, we might as well laugh as cry. Future travel brochures for our town could read: "Spend fun days counting Portland's trash go by!"

Or how about livening the scenery while traveling between the endless loads of city dregs with quick, short signs like the old Burma Shave?

Drive the Gorge / in too much haste,
You could end up / in Portland's waste.

Aug. 9, 1989

—〇З—

A JOY FOR THE WOMAN WHO
WASN'T BORN YESTERDAY —

shoes by Reebok, Nike and the others, and fashion's permission to wear them, well, almost anywhere. In the advertising profession years ago we called all comfortable, sensible, low-heeled styles for women "old ladies' running shoes." Now that was prophetic.

Sept. 27, 1989

— ⊄ℛ —

CHAPTER 6

HOLIDAYS, SCHMOLIDAYS

— *Remembering the special times*

Explaining the jolly old guy

One good thing about this age of atomic miracles, supersonic speed and flying saucer mysteries—it makes a bit easier the explanation of how Santa gets into a house where there isn't any fireplace.

Dec. 11, 1953

—◌⳾◌—

Source of good manners

Usually talkative little visitor, being complimented on her fine behavior during auntie's Christmas dinner, replies, "Well, Mother, if you had such good food at home, I'd never talk at the table!"

Resolution keeping

Local philosopher says … keeping one good resolution for even a day is better than the thousand resolutions never made! Happy New Year!

Jan. 1, 1954

—◌⳾◌—

Mondegreens, part 1

Can you add to our collections of "mondegreens"? These, inspired by an article in the November 1954 Harper's, are scrambled versions of familiar phrases and songs. Usually they are the non-reading child's interpretation of adults' poor enunciation.

Samples: "With the jellied toast proclaim" … and "While shepherds washed their socks by night."

(continued)

Then, there is that wondrous flash illuminating the Star Spangled Banner above the rocket's red blare. It must have something to do with the mighty eight-bomb. It is the famous "Donzerly Light"!

July 1, 1955

— ∞ —

CREDIT CHRISTMAS

What price Christmas! Now that the big retail outlets generously urge customers to buy gifts and take 12 months to pay, greeting cards will have to come out with some new sentiments. Sample:

> Dear Sister, here's a gift for you –
> I have 12 months to pay the store –
> And if I meet installments due,
> Next Christmas I'll give you
> Something more!

Nov. 4, 1955

— ∞ —

CHRISTMAS WARNING

> Almost any woman
>   Is flattered by "Shocking,"
> Or "Breathless" or "Jet"
>   In her Christmas stocking.
> But look again, dear lady,
>   And brace your little selve …
> Instead of Chanel No. 5
>   You may get channel 12!

Dec. 16, 1955

— ∞ —

SHEPHERDS WATCHED THEIR FROCKS

Like old friends, there are bathrobes in this town which reappear year after year, practically from generation unto generation, in the Sunday school Christmas pageants. The nativity scene wouldn't be complete without them. Faces change and the shepherds grow up, but the familiar old bathrobes just keep coming back each Christmas!

Dec. 27, 1956

HOLIDAY REFLECTIONS

Meanest gift of the TV giveaway season: 1959 Cadillac windshield wiper!

To paraphrase a quotation: If you don't get everything you want for Christmas, think of the things you didn't get which you wouldn't want anyhow.

Have you remembered the birds' Christmas? They're not a bit fussy. Crusts from the bread stuffing . . . a piece of suet . . . oatmeal . . . chick scratch . . . bits of old apple for the robins.

December 1958

— ℞ —

SOME THINGS NEVER CHANGE

It proves there is still hope — when we keep making the same resolutions each New Year!

Jan. 1, 1959

— ℞ —

Angel Visitation

Friend tells of a Christmas program in a nearby school. Shortage of girls forced some little boys to take "angel" parts, complete with wobbly wings, the construction of which had been quite a headache to the mothers.

The Christmas drama was getting under way when a late-comer inadvertently let a dog into the classroom. Dog spotted his master in spite of the angel disguise and forthwith greeted the little boy with puppy abandon. The erstwhile angel went down in a hodge-podge of broken wings, flailing paws and puppy kisses. The sober Christmas play broke up then and there!

Dec. 10, 1959

— ଘ —

Wise, Indeed

Gentleman who overheard this says he's sure it wasn't meant to be sacrilegious. Two rather youngish boys were walking up Oak street when one turned back toward the nativity scene on the U.S. National bank lawn. "I want to see those Three Wise Guys again," he said.

Dec. 24, 1959

— ଘ —

Dateline Decembah

Deck the halls with Kleenex,
Fill the house with Vick,
Pass the nosedrops, Harold,
And the vaporizer, quick!
Those noises in your head
Are not the carolers singing,
It's music of the winter cold
That sets your ears to ringing!

Leave aspirin for Santa Claus
And a double face mask, too.
Tell him not to breathe in here
Or else he'll get the flu;
When planning Christmas dinner,
Don't make it very fillin'
By then you may be stuffed
With misery and penicillin!

NEEDY DEFINED

Before Thanksgiving, a teacher here suggested that her class help a needy family.

"You're needy, too," said one boy to her.

"I am?"

"Yes, you live with 32 children in one room!"

Dec. 15, 1960

FOR A CHANGE

Oh say, did you see
  Last Thursday's blue sky?
A time to remember ...
  A nice Fourth of July!

July 4, 1963

IT'S ALL IN THE WRAPPING

Bet you women old enough to remember thought of the good old days when all Christmas packages were wrapped in white tissue paper, tied with green, red or white ribbon and dotted with colorful stickers. There wasn't any other way to tie up a present.

(continued)

Now, egged on by the elaborate gift packages in how-to-do-it magazines, wrapping the presents has taken on more importance than the gifts themselves, and costs as much.

Are the papers and ribbons properly coordinated? How was it you learned to make that double-donged, triple bell out of stickum ribbon last year? Are we out of the tags that match this cerise foil paper?

Talk about frustrations, and decisions, piled one upon the other. In the precious time before Christmas, you sit with booklet entitled "How to Create Glamorous Gift Packages" propped up in front of you as small, hot tears trickle down over the rubber cement, glue, sticky tape, scissors and snips of ribbon.

The results, unless you are artistic and sensitive, looked like something the dog dragged home. And who took time to admire your loving handiwork Christmas morn? Well, you did.

Jan. 2, 1964

—ℭ—

CHRISTMAS TRUISMS

How better to describe the time of Christmas than by snatches of conversation. Some of it you said, some we said, some of it was unsaid but obvious.

> Every time I pick out a good Christmas recipe, it's too fattening, so I go back to the same old ones. Come to think of it, they're fattening, too.

> Me? Oh, I don't want anything. Maybe just a box of razor blades I can call my own.

> One thing we always will do, no matter what — put a candle in the window just in case Somebody is out there.

> If you object to the size of your Christmas card list, quit making friends next year.

Bless her heart! All she wants is snow and a look at the Star.

Every time I pick out a good Christmas recipe it calls for some fancy stuff like saffron or Cognac or kumquats and those things I don't keep on MY shelves so I go back to the same old cookies and fruit cake.

When I got through I had so much money in the wrappings they made the gift look cheap.

Mama, Sheila's folks are giving her — you don't CARE what Sheila's folks are giving her for Christmas?

That fir stood in the woods heaven knows how many years making all this good green and now you want to spray it PURPLE?

Best Christmas we ever had. Popcorn strings, paper chains, pinecones, fir boughs, and didn't cost a cent.

It isn't half so much fun giving when everyone has everything as it was when none of us had anything.

I can't save enough out of my LITTLE allowance for the REALLY nice gift I'd LIKE to give you and dad!

Dec. 23, 1965

— ℭℜ —

SWELLING THE DUCK

Charlotte Perry told us of an episode on the Today program which suggested a way a small Thanksgiving bird can be s-t-r-e-t-c-h-e-d to serve more diners than originally expected. This particular fowl was a six-pound duck, cooked Chinese-style.

(continued)

You simmer it first in equal parts of soy sauce and sherry, and then bake and baste. And, suggested the cook, if you keep adding the sherry, a six-pound duck will eventually serve 20 people.

PACKAGE FOR THE BRIDE

Thanksgiving shopping list for the bride's first holiday dinner:

> One turkey — oven ready with thermometer that pops out when bird is done.
>
> Box of stuffing — seasoned and all set for the turkey.
>
> Can of consommé — only needs chilling.
>
> Can of cranberry sauce.
>
> Rolls — to be heated.
>
> Instant mashed potatoes or frozen yam casserole.
>
> Frozen creamed broccoli.
>
> Waldorf salad — delicatessen section.
>
> Mince pie — bakery section.
>
> Canned brandy sauce — just heat and add real brandy.
>
> Instant coffee.

BLESS THIS HOUSE

> "Chestnut stuffing! Now that's my bag."
>
> "To be perfectly truthful, I would have to say this dinner is 'home-heated.'"
>
> "Now that you're all here, I have news for you. I forgot to turn on the oven this morning."

"The little thermometer inside, it didn't pop out when it was done, so you'll find the turkey is done done."

"I wish Grandma liked football, so I could get her out of the kitchen."

"What does the Supreme Court say about giving thanks on Thanksgiving?"

"Pretty soon they're going to raise turkeys with nothing but breast. No wings, no legs, just all breast."

"How should I know where you keep the pickle fork? We haven't used it since last Christmas."

"Mama, I saw Grandpa pouring more brandy in the sauce."

"Where's the toothpicks? My mother always had a toothpick jar on the table. I don't care if they aren't polite. I've got turkey in my teeth."

"I told him, 'You can jolly well bet you have to wear your suit coat at the table.'"

"Why didn't he think to sharpen the carving knife sooner: The turkey's getting cold."

"You'd think they could do without football on TV this one day."

"Remember how we used to spend the day before, taking pinfeathers out with eyebrow tweezers?"

"No, you may NOT eat in front of the TV."

"And a thankful Thanksgiving to you all!"

Nov. 28, 1968

— ભ —

MONDEGREENS, PART 2

It's that time of year for mondegreens. Don't ask where the name came from. It's too long a story.

Mondegreens are the perfectly honest misinterpretations by children of words they have learned by ear. Christmas carols or hymns are the best sources:

> "We three kings of Oregon are …"

> "Wreck the halls with bowls of holly …"

Then there were the kindergartners preparing Nativity scenes for Christmas. One child, in addition to the Holy Family, added a fourth figure. To the teacher's question about his portly character, he replied, "Why that's Round John Virgin."

Dec. 19, 1968

— ❧ —

OBSERVING THE NEW YEAR

The ONLY concession to the New Year we make is to run around January first and sharpen all the pencils in the house. It may not improve the writing, but it certainly makes us feel neat for a day or two.

January 1970

— ❧ —

NEW YEARS OF YORE

In the 120 years since the first attempt to settle Hood River, most New Years Days in the valley have been quite ordinary. A few of them set weather records for better or worse. The bad ones gave people something to talk about for years, and left their mark on local history.

January 1, 1853

Weather very cold, with crust of ice over heavy snow since early November.

About 1,000 head of starving cattle milled around the log cabin of the William C. Laughlin family 12th and State streets today. The only other white family was that of a Dr. Farnsworth of the present location of Paradise motel.

All but 14 of the animals died. Mr. Farnsworth hewed out a large canoe and pulled away in January. The Laughlins stayed until April, when they returned to The Dalles.

January 1, 1855

Very mild weather. The Nathaniel Coe family was living in the abandoned Laughlin log cabin on their Donation Land Claim which covered most of the present site of the city.

On New Years Day they went by boat to have chicken dinner with Mr. and Mrs. Erastus Joslyn across the Columbia at what is now Bingen. The Joslyns were the only white people on the north side of the river between The Dalles and the Cascades.

Henry Coe wrote, "Such a glorious day and such a glorious dinner. The mountains were covered with grass and the ground blooming with bluebells and buttercups." The latter statement is a bit hard to believe.

January 1, 1856

ushered in an ordinary winter. The previous year — their first full year here — had been a good one for the Coes. The roothouse and cellars were filled, the barn bulged with hay, grain, corn and fodder, the young orchard was beginning to take hold.

In Washington Territory, the powerful Yakima Indian nation simmered with hatred toward the white men. Settlers on the Oregon side of the Columbia, although under the "protection" of troops at Fort Dalles, felt uneasy.

(continued)

When 12-year-old Henry Coe herded the family cattle to pasture in what is now downtown Hood River or worked the oxen in the field, he carried a rifle in one hand.

The Cascades massacre was to come in March.

January 1, 1859

The Coes entertained at dinner in the home they had now built.

Guests were Nathan and Martha Benson, who homesteaded on the east side of the Hood River near its mouth then called Dog river; newlyweds James and Margaret Benson, living on Indian creek; and the Sherman B. Ives, first settlers on the west side of the Lower Valley.

January 1, 1862

Snow had begun Nov. 19, remaining on the ground until April 12. Seven feet fell, with over four feet on the level at one time. Temperature reached 24 degrees below zero later in January.

The Columbia river closed to navigation on New Years Day. The steamer Idaho went down to the Cascades, its last trip until March 4.

Henry Coe, then 18 years old, boarded the Idaho at Hood River, bound for Portland to get medicine for a sick brother. The lower river was also closed, so he and a Wells Fargo messenger piloted a small boat through drift ice to the mouth of the Sandy river. From there they walked into Portland.

Henry returned to Hood River on foot through the Gorge, starting Jan. 6. Fresh snow piled up to two feet on top of old snow. The walk took three days.

January 1, 1884

brought more snow, which had been falling continuously since Dec. 13. Total depth on New Years Day, five feet. No roads were open. The only transportation was by snowshoes.

A combined passenger train from The Dalles stood west of Viento, caught in snowdrifts since Dec. 18. It remained there with 148 people aboard until rescued Jan. 7. Men from Hood River took supplies to the stranded train by snowshoe and sled.

On New Years Day, hopes of rescue were dampened when a 900-foot snow slide occurred at Mitchell Point to further imprison the train, several snow ploughs and nine "rescue" locomotives.

January 1, 1920

Hood River Valley was locked in by cold and snow. Temperatures had dropped to 30 below during December. Many apple trees were already dead and stored fruit frozen, in spite of valiant efforts to keep apple houses heated. The Columbia river was frozen solid.

January 1, 1921

The valley was deep in a winter worse than the previous year. There were no New Years celebrations. Hood River had been cut off from the rest of the world by a "tapioca" snow starting Nov. 19.

Many motorists were trapped on the highway at Shell Rock mountain. For nearly a mile the road was buried under tapioca snowdrifts, some of them 49 feet deep. Trains were halted. A steamer broke through from Portland to rescue those who had been caught on the highway.

Near-zero temperature and snow continued well into 1922.

January 1, 1972

Happy New Year!

Dec. 29, 1971

— ❧ —

MERRY CHRISTMAS FROM HOOD RIVER

TO THE WOBBLY OLD WORLD

The OPF Christmas tape recorder broke down this year. Instead of picking up happy snatches of conversation, it overloaded with static about high prices … slow mail … lousy rain … power problems … ethics in high places and where can you buy fireplace wood.

The tape finally snapped under the weight of the groans it was recording. The last smothered comment was, "I'd like to be back in the good old days this Christmas!"

So back you go. The past always seems pleasanter.

Christmas 1852

Sitting in their barricaded log cabin in what is now the heart of Hood River city, the William Laughlin family held Christmas services while a thousand head of bawling, starving cattle milled around outside, literally dying at the door. Ice-crusted snow had covered their pasturage since November.

When the Laughlins left in the spring, only 14 cattle and the family milk cow remained alive. That was a Christmas to remember!

Christmas 1854

The Nathaniel Coe family observed their first Christmas here in that same log cabin. There is no mention of gifts in the Coe diaries. Only religious services at home.

They may have had a little extra for dinner on the Day — duck or goose bought from one of the other four white settlers. They paid Indians fifty cents for a deer.

An energy crisis developed in the Coe cabin that first winter. The supply of candles had given out. Pitch pine torches lit up the one room, but covered food and bed clothing with soot.

"We gave up the idea of light and sat out the long winter evenings in the dark."

Christmas 1861

The James Bensons invited the Coes to dinner in their log cabin on Indian creek.

This home was elegant by the standards of some 60 people then living in Hood River Valley. It had not the usual puncheon floor of rough-dressed timber, the flat side up, but regular flooring lumber imported from Portland.

The table was a piece of 16-inch planking left over from the floor. Covered with four immaculate flour sacks, it was so high and the improvised chairs so low that the Christmas victuals were close to mouths.

Terrible weather now, you say?

That Christmas 1861 was the worst winter here until 1919-20. Snow had started falling Nov. 19. It lasted until April 22, at times reaching five to eight feet on the level.

When it did not snow, it rained. Rivers flooded all over western Oregon. By Christmas day the ice-jammed Columbia closed to steamers, the only connection between Hood River and the outside world.

The Bensons raised cattle along Indian Creek. To keep them from starving, they were fed every bit of hay, grain and flour on the farm, even the straw bed ticking in a mattress Mrs. Benson had made from 13 flour sacks.

Christmas 1884

On the Great Day, 148 passengers and the crews of four trains coupled together, westbound, had been stalled at present Starvation Creek for eight days.

Christmas dinner was brought to the marooned train by 12 men walking the tracks from Cascade Locks. Bacon, beans, canned fruit, pickles and coffee. The cooking was done alongside the train, which did not move for three weeks.

(continued)

Hood River people emptied their own shelves to send provisions by snowshoe and sled to the imprisoned train. They, too, were immobilized. The snow was piling up in the valley, reaching 12 feet at one time.

Neighbors who could reach each other traded cornmeal and pork for butter and milk. Flour and sugar gave out.

They had shortages then, too!

Mrs. Alma Howe wrote of that 1884 Christmas, "We were without lights … Coal oil lamps had been our only lights, then candles … Many had to use fences and cut down trees for wood. Some stayed in bed more than they wanted to, to keep warm … It was years before I wanted to taste cornbread again!"

Christmas in the 1890s

got little mention in the new Hood River Glacier. In those times the day meant worship services, a program and a potluck dinner in one of the few churches here.

Gifts were simple, and scarce. Of course Santa got around, but even he was hard up then.

"The most welcome Christmas present

you could make the editor would be to come in and settle arrearages and pay for a year in advance," commented the Glacier.

Very likely, the subscriptions were paid in farm produce or wood. Trading took the place of cash, which was seldom seen.

Flour was 95 cents a sack, $3.75 the barrel. You could buy felt slippers for 50 cents, stamped doilies for 2-1/2 cents each. Leggings and over gaiters were 25 to 35 cents.

Those were "the good old days"?

Most of the years tottered along from problem to problem, from disaster to disaster, with Christmas a one-day rest from the struggle to survive — the hard way.

Now, would you really want to go back?

Merry Christmas and may your Scotch tape hold everything together through the holidays!

Dec. 20, 1973

— ℞ —

SETTLERS' THANKSGIVING

It can't be stated with certainty that the first white settlers took time off to observe Thanksgiving during their first busy autumn in Dog River (Hood River). Not a whole day. Few did then.

There probably was a special Thanksgiving meal because these people were first-comers themselves.

One of the few references in the Coe journals occurred Nov. 22, 1858: "Indian shot a drake. We cooked a swan. Called it Thanksgiving dinner."

Nov. 27, 1975

— ℞ —

HONORING THE FLAG AS CIVIL WAR RAGES

The Fourth of July shouldn't pass without a thought for the most colorful historic event to occur in Hood River.

It was 1861, seven years after the first permanent white settlers arrived. On April 14 the Civil War started with the shelling of Fort Sumpter. The news trickled into the tiny Hood River settlement weeks later, inspiring a memorable Fourth of July celebration.

Even in the new west feeling ran high about abolition of slavery. The Nathaniel Coes, who had led the first four families here in 1854, were from New York state, sympathetic to the Northern cause and loyal to the new president, Abraham Lincoln. Coe had fought in the War of 1812.

(continued)

On June 21 the few white settlers met at Nathan Benson's cabin on the east side of the Hood river. They decided that there must be a special Fourth of July here in this wilderness. But without an American flag? Unthinkable!

A few days later patriarch Coe himself went by sternwheeler to the Cascades, made the portage and continued on to Portland by another steamer, no easy trip. There he bought material for a flag and returned to Hood River.

On June 26 Coe took the bunting, cut into stripes and a blue field, to Miss Corinne Moody in The Dalles. She assembled the flag on the first sewing machine brought to that part of Oregon.

At home the handful of women in the settlement cut out 34 white stars which they stitched onto the field.

They were Mrs. Coe, two Mrs. Bensons, Phila Jenkins, Julia Birnie and Candace Griswold, whose husband had been killed during the Cascades massacre of 1856.

The 34 stars were not perfectly shaped, nor was the one big star they were meant to form accurate in dimensions, but no matter. At that time there existed no standard design for the American flag.

Says the Coe farm diary, "June 30 — Raised flag pole."

The site chosen was a pretty grove of oak trees on what is now L.B. Gibson park, the former location of Park Street school in the heart of Hood River. It was then on the Coe Donation Land Claim farm.

According to Coe writings, "a bower was built; tables, chairs, seats made and a flag pole erected."

Fourth of July 1861 arrived and the Coes methodically noted what kind of a day it was, as they did for many years:

> "50 sunrise, 73 extreme. 72 sunset — wind up.
> Flying clouds."

The handmade American flag, 8 by 12 feet in size, was flying, too.

"July 4 — Pic-nic. Celebration — about 32 persons present."

Thus the brief Coe diary entry concerning the first real celebration of the Fourth in Hood River.

> Promptly at 10 a.m. there in the clearing among the oaks, all present stood silently as the homemade flag was hauled to the masthead. Nathaniel Coe took hold of the halyards that bound the flag in a roll and "our beautiful new flag floated free in the western breeze."

Stand fast for the Union

Imagine the thrill for those patriotic hearts, the sight of the Stars and Stripes flying for the first time over this isolated settlement so far from their old homes and the nation's capital.

Three rousing cheers went up, followed by a "tiger." Then they sang the Star Spangled Banner. Sherman Ives delivered "a stirring oration exhorting all to stand fast in their loyalty to the Union" and Erasmus Joslyn of Bingen, as chaplain, no doubt contributed a prayer for a quick end to the war. Dinner and a "social good time" followed, there in the oak grove.

Henry Coe took the old flag with him when he left for California many years later, but in 1924 he returned it "into the keeping of the citizens of Hood River."

So now the old flag hangs folded and behind glass in the council chambers, almost unnoticed. Some day it ought to be allowed to stretch its full size in a fitting place where all could see how the pioneers of 1861 declared their patriotism.

As a footnote, Arthur Roberts of Portland tells us that his grandparents, renting a farm from the Joslyns in Bingen and living for a while in the government blockhouse, could see the big flag

(continued)

flying on a hillside in Hood River. His own father, then a small boy, told of seeing it at half-mast one day, in 1865, and it was some time before the Roberts heard why — President Lincoln had been assassinated.

June 30, 1966, and July 1, 1976

— ∝ —

REFLECTIONS OF THE CHRISTMAS SEASON

"About this time of year, when I start calling everyone in the family by their full given names, they know it's time to shape up and help more."

"Saved her little allowance and went shopping. When she came home she said, "You know, I've decided that money is very expensive."

"I'm trying to think of a subtle way I can let him know that I'd rather have a crock pot than another negligee."

"She asked me how old Santa Claus is. She's afraid he's about ready to retire on his Social Security."

Dec. 15, 1977

— ∝ —

CHRISTMAS IS BORN

On Sunday, a Hood River physician had an early call. He delivered a baby, then joined the choir at his church to sing the Bach Christmas cantata, "To Us a Child Is Given."

Jan. 3, 1980

— ∝ —

HALLOWEEN LOGIC

Backtracking through this column: A few years ago three trick-or-treaters at the door appeared outsize for such Halloween activity.

"Isn't this about your last year?" we asked. Replied the tallest one,
"We may be BIG, but we think small!"

Oct. 20, 1990

—∞—

Pilgrims' progress

The feasting time is over –
  May all have had their fill
Of fine old American cooking,
  With tidbits to use up still;

There was plump, broad-breasted turkey
  Pan-readied for the oven
And from a box came all prepared
  Ingredients for the stuffin';

A feast processed and pasteurized
  With nation-wide display
Of modern know-how, including too,
  The pills for after-meal dismay!

(Date unknown)

—∞—

CHAPTER 7

AROUND THE HEARTH

— Family and home memories

HOME EFFICIENCY AN OXYMORON

Much as we admire efficiency experts there comes a mean little hunch that it is a long haul between theory and practice.

Take the case of home management. They keep telling us that we should make a bed in 23 steps and four minutes. And that a meal can be prepared with slightly over 400 steps, provided the kitchen is properly planned. Undoubtedly they even have certified proof of these facts, but we'll wager they were accomplished in a soundproof test laboratory behind locked doors.

No phone calls to make or take; no yelling, "Hey, Mom, can you come here a minute?"; no confusions; no emergency errands — all of which turn bed making into a major operation and meal preparation into a mile trot!

Jan. 14, 1955

— Ꮗ —

MARBLE NAMES

If you possess young sons, your conversation must be properly geared to the season. Right now it's "clearies," "cat eyes," "steelies," "date-ins" and "boulders" — strict classification of marbles, we gather. It is also the time when the good knees in jeans become things of the past.

Feb. 18, 1955

— Ꮗ —

SUNSHINE'S BLESSINGS AND CURSES

This time of year home managers experience two emotions: 1, joy at the slightest patches of sunlight and 2, horror at what the sunshine reveals of our winter housekeeping!

March 11, 1955

— Ꮗ —

Persona non-gratis

Ever been persona non-gratis in your own household? That's us when it comes to marbles. Ol' knuckles cleans up on 'em every time. Man or boy, they can't accept that!

April 8, 1955

— ∞ —

It's simple, mom

A lesson from the littlest one: "You know how spring works, mama! I think we put the seeds in the ground. Then God holds them in his hand so they'll grow and grow!"

April 15, 1955

— ∞ —

Flower joy

Every mother faces this dilemma sometime: What to do when the littlest one proudly presents a bouquet of your choicest blooms urgently stripped from the flower garden?

June 10, 1955

— ∞ —

Where's the food?

The usher handed Grandmother a program as she and little missy six-year-old enter the church. When they were seated, Miss Six whispered, "Where's my menu, Grandma?"

RIP Dickie

To his many admiring friends, a simple announcement: Master Richard has left for the land of eternal catnip.

An obituary for Dickie has been on the tip of our tongues many times over the years, but the big fellow always pulled through. This time he must have been traveling on thin ice of his ninth and last life.

Gentle as an old tabby at home, he was a demon out in his own world. As he probably would have wanted it, his last fight was a great one, according to those who heard it. Like the Gingham Dog and the Calico Cat, they literally "ate each other up!" At least, it was an honorable sort of death for the big cat!

July 22, 1955

— ∝ —

FILTHY LUCRE, INDEED

Most oft repeated question from the littlest one: "Do you wish money grew on trees?"

The "no" answer and subsequent lesson on supply and demand, diminishing returns and economics in general falls flat on its face before that fascinating dream we all have had at some time — an endless supply of filthy lucre!

Feb. 17, 1957

— ∝ —

DISNEYLAND, USA

Here is the ideal way to arrive at the main gate of this highly publicized domain after parking your car in the 10,000-car lot … Lagging behind excited children … Knowing absolutely nothing about the place nor what to expect … Regretting the loss of a whole precious vacation day … Loathing Mickey Mouse and all his kinfolk … Wondering if you'll have enough money left to get home again, after all the tales about two people spending $30, $40 or even $100 at Disneyland!

(continued)

Because after passing through that main gate, Disneyland opens up into a vista of yesterday, tomorrow, dreamland and adventure magic no adult can resist if he has an ounce of nostalgia or imagination or childlike wonder in his bones. What a marvelous surprise it is! Disneyland is for everyone, and the glimpse of Mickey Mouse we had was the outline of a silly little face done in living flowers below the train station.

Those tales about the stupendous sums to be spent in Disneyland are fantastic. But they scared us before we arrived, what with the children holding their modest hard-earned cash outlay in their hot hands. We'd heard that one woman spent $40 on herself and small girl in a day. Well, she must have included hotel accommodations and expensive souvenirs for all the family in that amount. The trip need not be that expensive. The average cost of a visit to Disneyland is reported to be $2.29. We can believe it. At the ticket office books of scrip are obtainable, the most expensive being $3.00 for children, $3.50 for juniors and adults $4.00. This gives one a choice of 15 rides, amusements and exhibits in all sections of Disneyland and includes general admission to the magic kingdom. And it takes all day to use up a book of scrip, going at full pace. The unused scrip may be saved for another day. A number of exhibits are free.

The right word for Disneyland doesn't come easily: Fabulous … terrific … stunning! The mere thought that three years ago this place was an orange grove in Anaheim, Cal., is itself a stopper. The splendid trees, shrubs, flowers and grass look as if they'd been there forever. Many of the trees were brought in full-grown, with generous forethought to shade on the hottest days. The buildings are permanent structures. There is nothing of the one-night-stand or carnival atmosphere about Disneyland, its amusements, its shops or its attendants. This is an ageless dreamland and we are glad, because we want to go back again someday.

Imagination is the keynote everywhere. Children catch the feel of it from the moment the main gates open into the main street of 1890 with its Emporium, its apothecary shop and 30 other old-time stores. Yet it is not only for the youngsters; it is for all the young in heart. Anyone should give up who doesn't get a kick out of the 2-1/2 mile trip on the Santa Fe & Disneyland RR ... the jungle river boat tour through honest-to-goodness, living tropical growth ... a voyage on the old time 105-foot sternwheeler ... the skyride high above the magic land ... the stagecoach journey through Frontierland ... the horse-drawn streetcars and surreys behind a giddy-hatted nag ... the raft ride to Tom Sawyer's island ... driving scaled down racers on miniature freeways.

Food need not be an expensive item. There are 24 places to eat, from open-air cafeterias, refreshment stands and dairy bars to more elaborate restaurants like the Red Wagon Inn and the Chicken Plantation ... The Monsanto House of the Future looks like a huge mushroom with its own air-cooling water and exotic water plants underneath the rooms, but it contains innovations we won't see in our own homes for years ... Fine artists and musicians entertain in the five sections of Disneyland ... When you go, plan to stay into the evening for cooler temperatures and magnificent lighting effects.

You go away from Disneyland feeling that delightful kingdom was conceived, not by a man who merely creates animated cartoons, but by men with great pride in the past, with a great and good sense of humor, with infinite attention to detail, with faith in the future and, most of all, with honest respect for the personal dignity of millions of Americans who will come to Disneyland with not more than $2.29 to spend!

July 25, 1957

— ❧ —

Valentine

Life may be a fat bowl of cherries
    for certain optimistic Tom, Dick and Marys,
But for most of us it has ups and downs,
    with plenty of laughter and some irritable sounds.
And since I've no desire to live with a saint,
    I'm happy with you as you are — and not as you ain't.

— ❧ —

Love is patient —

It pays to be married to a good-natured man. Especially when you forget the picnic meat, main course, which means a 15-mile trip back home for him!

July 9, 1959

— ∞ —

Taking it literally

Childhood impressions revealed: Just-under-teen confesses that, before she could read, she used to look at that long thing called Lincoln's Gettysburg Address and wonder how you would ever get it all on an envelope!

Sept. 22, 1960

— ∞ —

Truth in advertising

Here's a reassuring fact for those who may doubt what they see on commercial TV.

Kenneth McClain [Ruth's brother], HRHS '22, before his retirement from Proctor and Gamble, invested and was responsible many years for all phases of Comet cleaner.

When Josephine the lady plumber used Comet on a sink stain, the demonstration had to be authentic, with real stains and honest results in the studio when the commercial was made.

On one occasion before the cameras, Comet failed to remove a stain better than its competitive X brand. Ken hurried to New York, discovered that some chemical being added to the water in the building had disarmed his product of its cleaning ability.

Regular water was used and Josephine and her Comet sailed through the TV film strip, a winner once again.

August 1971

— ⍶ —

Grace Fehl McClain

People prepare for trips in different ways. Some with fear, wishing they could stay home. Some quietly, at the ready, excited, expecting a wonderful time. My mother was one of the latter, ready for that final journey. She had made her reservations years before and she had begun to think that the Travel Agent had forgotten her. Most of her friends had gone ahead of her.

But then the call came for the big trip and she was ready. Her bag was neatly packed, you might say, and she must have settled back with a sigh of relief when the Conductor finally took her ticket.

She never doubted that this would be a splendid adventure. Her Christian faith was unshakable, unquenchable. It began with good, old-fashioned Methodism, detoured by marriage to Congregationalism but never wavered from the certainty that the best was yet to come.

In her later years she often said, "Don't wish to live this long." But if she had been the one to make the choice — and perhaps she was — she would likely have stayed exactly as long as she did, 97 years.

Because, if life slowed down for her after 90 and she saw it more dimly and heard it less clearly, she still enjoyed the stream of it flowing around her. She tried hard to be flexible, to understand and accept the changing scene. She never lectured on how much better things were in her day, even if she may have been tempted to do so.

To the very last this little woman blessed her lucky stars that she had been able to carry on under her own steam, even when the

(continued)

—157—

power plant wavered toward the end. She maintained her own apartment, she took care of her business matters, she cooked her own well-balanced meals, and every day she said a prayer of thanks for the strength and will that let her do so.

Best of all, she had no fear of the final journey, only joyful anticipation of what she expected it to be like. What a wonderful way to go.

1976

— ❧ —

Growing pains

Concerned when her 14-year-old son developed a hoarse, rasping voice, a relative of ours plied him with cold remedies and vitamin C. After three weeks without improvement, she came to. His voice was changing.

Jan. 22, 1986

— ❧ —

Poetry through the years for loved ones

Message for a daughter

Among the things I'll leave
When at last I die –
Ten thousand cut-out recipes
I always meant to try.

For my father

How like him
   to die
while summer laughter
   lingered in the
   brittle leaves.

On graduating

Rarely a rosebud
so promising
— sweet, pale pink?
No! rich red,
I think!

Boy joy

World unfurled:
Sights, delights.
Explain Spain,
Define Einstein.
Ug slug,
Mice, nice;
Sun, fun,
Rain, pain;
Nickel, popsicle,
Deploys toys,
Enjoys noise;
Tub, sub;
Ears, tears;
Soap, mopes;

Bad — he's Dad's;
Fine — he's mine!

Signs of growth

To clean the smudgy fingerprints –
    Dirt, chocolate and paste –
I used to genuflect and bend
    To levels below the waist.
The telltale marks still reappear
    On woodwork and on wall.
Except that, in the years between,
    Those prints have grown tall.

(continued)

And where they once were evidence
    Of mud pies and such toil,
They now consist of axle grease,
    Peanut butter and motor oil!

Snow boy

You love the snow? Oh, little boy,
That proves your young and tender years;
Too soon you'll take your winter joy
Before the fireplace, toasting your arrears!

— ❦ —

CHAPTER 8

GRINS, GIGGLES AND GUFFAWS

— Hood River humor

LIFE'S-LITTLE-FRUSTRATIONS DEPT.

Friend, busy canning and jelly-making, says it drives her crazy trying to fit dill pickles into quart jars!

JUST DUCKY

Can't resist telling this one on the editor. Jack [Travis] agreed to board and room ten large ducklings and their mother for a while this Summer. Arriving home at 11 p.m. with his guests in three large gunnysacks, he unloaded the first batch in a specially enclosed section of his creek.

When he returned with the rest, no ducks! Instead, loud, lonesome quacks somewhere out in the night. He found his charges hot-footing it up Montello Avenue and onto Jim Ocheltree's front porch. By the time he rounded them up, the rest of the ducks had escaped and it was midnight.

Jack, sweating over thoughts of being lodged in the city bunkhouse for maintaining a public nuisance, finally corralled all 11 ducks permanently — with the help of the neighborhood, mostly in its nightclothes. The Travises have decided that newspaper work has fewer hazards than babysitting for ducks!

January 1951, Hood River Daily Sun

— ❧ —

DOWNTOWN BARE FEET

As I hear it, Tom Scott was the first to spot him early one morning at the post office, and the sight left Tom dumfounded. It was a man, obviously a tourist, dressed in a red striped shirt, shorts … and he came paddling along the hot sidewalk in his big bare feet!

Comfortable crowding

See where the Bonneville Power Administration will be cozily installed in a $3,250,000 building in a year or so. A good thing it is too. When I did business with the BPA some years ago in its present location, the place was so crowded the men kept their feet on their desks all the time!

All work

Friend had a good idea all figured out for the Civic Theatre's radio script contest. It was to be a play with a snappy title, "All Work and No Play." You guessed it! She was too busy to get the script written ... all work, no play!

Bed with a past

This will turn antique collectors slightly green! A young couple who lived here for a while owned a most peculiar-looking bed. It was a mongrel — neither period piece nor modern. Asked about it, the couple explained that it was an old four-poster, a family heirloom which had originally come around the Horn. Not caring for the canopy or the mahogany, they had sawed off the posts and painted the bed white!

Aug. 27, 1951, Hood River Daily Sun

— CR —

What to do with half an egg?

Mary (Mrs. Tony) Mohr, an avid collector of china and antiques, is keeping an eagle eye out for one special dish. It provokes her to find that all egg plates she ever saw or owned had 15 scallops for the devilled eggs. She's making it her goal in life to find one with an even number of grooves so she won't have to fix 7-1/2 eggs. It's the half of an egg that bothers her. That's the one for the cook, Mary!

Nov. 19, 1951, Hood River Daily Sun

— CR —

Remember Postum?

One of those why-didn't-I-think-of-it-first items: coffee-flavored Postum!

Feb. 18, 1955

— ભ —

Detergent dream

> New achievements in science
> And psychiatry give hope
> That some day we'll learn
> Why little boys hate soap!

April 15, 1955

— ભ —

Advice to the husbands of women

In spite of their efforts to make you think otherwise, the manner of women's endurance is quite a surprise. Their health is good and they seem quite at ease in automatic kitchens, in high heels and girdles that squeeze. They can stand babies' crying much better than men do. They pay no heed to jet planes nor a squeaky shoe. But there's one noise that makes women mentally shriek … it's the gentle pit, pit, pit, of faucets that leak!

April 29, 1955

— ભ —

City bargain

It is to laugh! Friend proudly purchased small handful of watercress in the city market for 35 cents. Toted it home in withered condition, only to be told that the wet cliffs along the top

(continued)

of Ruthton hill west of HR abound in the succulent stuff. And does it make a good green base for salads. Yum!

July 8, 1955

— ⌀ —

RICH KID

Heard of a man who was following a super deluxe Cadillac one day. A small hand stuck out of the back window of the Caddy was fluttering something in the breeze. Out of curiosity our man passed the big, sleek auto.

"I might have known it," he reported later. "The kid was waving a greenback!"

SEPTEMBER SHOWER

> In this first rainy shower
>   Our kind heart just bled
> For the guy trying to hoist
>   A convertible top over the head!

Sept. 16, 1955

— ⌀ —

APRIL VIGNETTE

> Spring has its own peculiar
>   sounds
>   Beside bird and bee wings
>   a-whirring …
> 'Tis the busy buzz of the little
>   flu bug,
>   And the political grass-roots
>   a-stirring!

April 5, 1956

— ⌀ —

Teenage emergency!

Hospitals are used to emergencies, but HR Memorial ran into a new one last week — and took care of it.

9 p.m. Footsteps in the quiet lobby. High school boy appears at reception desk. All dressed up. No sign of physical pain, but mental anguish apparent.

9:01 Says to receptionist, "Do you suppose you have a flower you could give me for my girl?"

9:02 Receptionist recovers from surprise. Asks questions. Boy is double-dating for Elks dance. Forgot corsage for his girl. Florist's closed. Couldn't think of anywhere to turn but to the hospital!

9:03 Staff alerted for emergency. Rooms of less ill patients searched. No flowers available for corsage.

9:10 Boy getting more nervous. Staff member Mrs. K. has inspiration. Phones Ray Calmettes. Sympathetic florist says sure he'll go over to the shop and make up a corsage.

9:13 Grateful boy leaves hospital headed for the greenhouse. Staff settles down to a routine night.

Jan. 7, 1960

— ◌ —

The Moses

Mother is telling little Miss Laurie Radliff the story of Moses in the bulrushes. Asks teeny tiny Laurie, who is up on the news, "Where was Grandma Moses?"

March 17, 1960

— ◌ —

Stocking the Bomb Shelter

Ultimate in optimists — the woman who includes hair tint in her stockpile list for the bomb shelter!

Nov. 1, 1962

— C3 —

Amazing Bird Transformation

The birds have appeared lackluster and colorless all winter, as we looked out on them. Suddenly they have regained their normal shading and hues — just since spring window cleaning!

Dog News

Well anyhow, dogs enjoy the society and club page of the News! Lois Talbot didn't know that she had a surprise one-man showing of her watercolors at Tucker's Studio until told about it some time after the printed announcement.

Seems Miss Ginger Snap, her father's dachshund pup, had taken the page from that week's issue to a quiet corner where she could digest the news!

March 23, 1961

— C3 —

Back to the Woolies

Dear diary: June 10 — turned off the furnace, put the snow shovel away. June 21 — stored the winter woolens. June 26 — Planted zucchini. June 28 — Started the furnace again and got out woolens to wear.

July 10, 1969

— C3 —

MISBEHAVIN'

"Wouldn't you think people would teach their kids to be better behaved than that?" screamed home-bound folks one recent night down on Oak and First street, over the obsessive blast of an auto horn. It was a shrill mixture of long blares followed by short bleats, then more long blats.

When discovered in a parked car, the "kid" turned out to be a poodle dog who looked just plain cross as it manipulated the horn.

A woman came charging out of the Mount Hood hotel and roundly scolded the poodly.

"I can't take this dog in the hotel!" she explained to onlookers, as if her pet should understand hotel rules.

Bystanders swore the poodle looked quite pleased with all of the attention.

March 16, 1972

— ❧ —

THE GOOD OLD DAYS

Young people wonder when were "the good old days"? They get as many answers as the number of people they ask.

Here's OPF's answer, culled from past columns:

The good old days were:

> When a hunting dog spotted the cash containers which then flew on wires to the J.C. Penney cashier. Dog went wild, jumped on the counters, barked madly after those featherless "birds."

> When the Hugh Shearers forgot to clean out the wrens' house for the spring arrival. The birds didn't show. Hugh

(continued)

later found them and a healthy nest of young — in the pocket of an old pair of overalls hanging outside his shop.

When a postcard collector found one dated 1900 showing Hood River's downtown Oak street. Wrote the sender, "This is an awful place. I wouldn't want to be caught dead here."

When the Percy Mansers had a wren house outside their window to which the male came every spring and tediously filled with nesting material. A week later, to the day, a lady wren arrived, looked over his work and said some sharp words to him. Then she threw every last thing he had gathered out the door and started over from scratch.

When a second-grade boy, writing his thank-you note to Norm Tucker for a class visit to the art studio, asked his teacher how to spell "nude." He had particularly noticed a painting of an unclothed woman, respectably turned away from the viewer. Teacher replied that she would rather he didn't use that word in the note. So he wrote, "Thanks for showing us the pictures. I sure did like the lady with her clothes off."

When Ned Marshall raised three Canadian goslings with permission of the state game commission. The baby honkers looked up to him as their daddy, followed him around the yard as he flapped his "wings" to the delight of his four children. When the agreed time for releasing them came, Ned took his charges to the Columbia, said a sentimental farewell and launched them — three times. They just climbed out of the water and waddled after "daddy." Finally, Ned spotted a slight current near shore, set his goslings a-sail on the outward-bound ripple and ran like anything to his car.

April 21, 1977

— CR —

Helping out the Energy Crisis

No kid, they are not urging us to save THAT kind of energy. Now get out there and rake the yard!"

One more item for our Dr. Edmundson collection

… and then we'll let him rest on his laurels, or whatever.

Sign posted on hospital bulletin board one time:
"DR. EDDY — PLEASE MUMBLE LOUDER!"

June 9. 1977

— ෬ —

Funny snippets

The ol' typewriter reached out and nipped me. It was going blind from disuse and summer heat. Rain peps it up.

So it's time to throw away all of the 90-degree notes, now out-weathered, except for these unforgettable memories:

Of the woman driving down Oak street using hot pads to grip a hot, hot steering wheel.

Of the young hitch-hiker whose sign said, "I'M SAFE."

Of the description of life in Russia today from an American woman who had resided there until recently. "It's the kind of situation where, if you saw a line, you got into it because you might be able to buy a couple of shriveled oranges."

Sept. 29, 1977

— ෬ —

Mystery solved ...

when Marie Marshall was asked why so many pioneer furniture stores had undertaking as a sideline.

Because, replied Marie whose father, Sam Bartmess, opened a furniture store here in 1891 and soon added undertaking, furniture stores were the only businesses with heavy lifting equipment and space to handle coffins. As simple as that.

May 10, 1979

— CR —

Accountant in training

Children get the hang of our paper money system very early nowadays.

Little boy not quite four wants candy at Keir's Drug Store. No, sez Mom, it's too close to dinner time. No money for candy.

"All right," announces not-quite-four. "I'll write my own check!"

Jan. 3, 1980

— CR —

No such "gentlemanly rivalry" ...

as we saw in the Winter Olympics existed in the days when Hood River and The Dalles used to compete as early as 1889 in baseball, and later, in high school games. Dirty tricks were commonplace.

After one game, The Dalles' team and rooters went back to their special railroad coach on a siding, to find it covered with good old Hood River mud.

Another time, Hood River fans followed a Dalles team to the train, pelting players with overripe vegetables and fruit. Maybe that was in 1914 when HRHS lost a football game to The Dalles 114 to 0.

Feb. 28, 1980

— Ɋ —

EVERY LITTLE OUNCE HELPS

One woman in Hood River is looking each day for even a few ounces' reduction in her weight, so she doesn't apply her makeup before stepping on the scales.

Another in the same boat has a predicament. Says she'd take off her glasses to lighten the load but then she couldn't see the scales. Dummy – weigh your glasses and then discount the ounces. Thanks. I'll do that.

May 8, 1980

— Ɋ —

HAPPY TO BE WASHINGTONIAN

Recent news report that a village in southern Oregon may be inside the California border reminds us of that elderly couple whose farm was in the northeastern corner of Oregon. When a new survey showed it to be in Washington, the man said, "I'm almighty glad, because I and the old lady couldn't have stood another one of those Oregon winters!"

Feb, 8, 1984

— Ɋ —

HISTORY ASIDE

The Glacier, Hood River's first newspaper started in 1889, strove for accuracy. An issue of 1893 had this item:

(continued)

Grand Recorder Newton Clark and Grand Officer Instructor Frank Day of the A.O.U.W. will deliver an address at the United Brethren church this Friday evening at 7 o'clock. This item is published tonight — that is, yesterday, so you need not expect to attend tonight, that is, tomorrow.

Feb. 7, 1990

— CR —

NUDGING OUR FUNNY BONE THROUGH THE YEARS

A better life?

Sometimes I wish I were my cat
Who scarcely cares where she is at;
She's not concerned with higher prices,
Her only interest is in fat mices;
She has no fear of income taxes
Or rheumatiz or appendix attackses.
But when she has a kitten she has eight ...
Now, what human wants that fate!

It's all in your point of view

You there, cat, with nothing much to do,
In moments of weakness we envy you;
Your worries limited to the number of mouses
Instead of taxes and bombproof houses;
The edge of the world measured by your meandering,
Your happiness dependent on the state of your
    philandering.
And yet, considering your life so exquisitely boring,
We'll stick to being human, for all its worry and warring.

Lines at the end of a bad day

"Spare the rod and spoil the child!"
    Such advice is rather mild;
A rod might do in days of yore
    But now it takes a two-by-four!

Shame on Caesar

February was an after-thought
　　To make the calendar slicker,
But all it did was make the bills
　　Come around two days quicker!

Dear Abby by electronics

When the status of U.S. marriages is computed
　　It may be that finances weren't what couples disputed
As much as the fact that he didn't say
　　"Your hair looks lovely tinted that way."
Or he forgot to mention that her packaged cake
　　Was better than cakes his mother used to bake;

Or in his blindness he naturally deduced
　　That her soft hands were from dishwasher use,
When his gentle whisper should have been,
　　"How much that new soap does for your skin!"
And she could ... have told him much oftener
　　That his after-shave lotion beckoned her,
Or have said, "It's your hair dressing, dear,
　　That saves our marriage year after year."

Actually, the only way to avoid a marriage adversial
　　Is to heed the advice of the TV commercial!

—ରେ—

KEY DATES IN HOOD RIVER'S HISTORY

1750 — Native people inhabit the Columbia Gorge, as they have for thousands of years. The Columbia River is a major transportation and trading route.

1805 — Lewis and Clark camp east of the mouth of the Hood River on way to Pacific Ocean. They name it the Labeasche River, bad spelling in honor of party member Francis Labiche.

1838 — Rev. Daniel Lee drives cattle across Hood River Valley from Oregon City to Methodist mission at The Dalles. It becomes the much-used Lee Cattle Trail.

1840s — Euro-Americans cross the country on the Oregon Trail to the Oregon Territory, passing what would become the cities of Hood River and Cascade Locks.

1843 — First Oregon Trail migrants float past on rafts or in Indian dugouts.

1851 — Sidewheeler James P. Flint steams upriver from the Cascades. Cascade Portage Railroad built to bypass the Cascades around present-day Cascade Locks.

1852 — In November William Laughlin and Dr. Farnsworth bring 500 cattle from The Dalles. Ice covers pasturage. Cattle die around log cabins on present site of city. Families leave.

1853 — Roger Atwell settles Cascade Locks by building a sawmill. Mary, a sidewheeler, is the first of several steamboats built in Cascade Locks.

1854 — Nathaniel Coe family, brothers Nathan and James Benson and the Walter Jenkins take out 320-acre claims close to the Hood River, then known as Dog River.

1858 — Dog River town renamed Hood River by Mary Coe. Six new families arrive in the valley. A.C. Phelps builds mill on creek to make oak kegs for whiskey going to gold mines.

(continued)

1860 — Peter Neal locates in valley, followed by Odell, Turner, Winchell and Divers. First census of Hood River is 70, not including children.

1861 — First U.S. flag flown in Hood River made by the Coe family.

1862 — In election at Coe home, 11 voters polled.

1863 — First schoolhouse in town built on present Belmont Road.

1866 — First bridge over Hood River constructed at a cost of $1,645.

1868 — Bachelors Steven Baldwin and A.H. Tieman homestead in Upper Valley.

1870 — Census shows 23 family homes and 85 people in the valley.

1875 — "Dog River peaches" being sold in The Dalles and Portland. Mansfield Pacific Colony of about 56 people arrive and settle in Barrett district.

1881 — Henry and Eugene Coe plat four blocks above proposed location of railroad line. Lots free to those who build immediately. Mount Hood Hotel and two stores go up. Schoolhouse built on lot given by Coes at present site of county courthouse.

1882 — Track of O.W.R.&N. Railroad completed through Hood River. It links the region with the East Coast. The first railroad depot in Hood River constructed.

1884-1885 —
Starvation Creek named when four westbound trains are stranded for three weeks with 148 persons on board. Food brought from Hood River by people on snowshoes.

1885 — T.R. Coon plants 200 Clark's seedling strawberries, leading to first large-scale shipments of fruit from the area.

1886 — Peter Mohr plants first dryland orchard with 400 apple trees near Odell. Captain John Stanley starts ferry service for wagons and passengers between Stanley Rock (Koberg's Beach) and White Salmon with barge and sailboard.

1887 — Captain Henry Coe's two small vessels, the Wasco and Irma, provide passage between The Dalles and Cascade Locks.

1889 — First Hood River newspaper, the "Hood River Glacier," is printed. Cloud Cap Inn opens in August.

1890s — Finnish immigrants begin settling in Oak Grove.

1891 — Hood River Townsite Company incorporated.

1893 — Hood River Fruit Growers Union, the first farmers' cooperative in the Pacific Northwest, organized for marketing fruit.

1895 — Hood River becomes a municipality.

1896 — Locks at Cascade Locks completed.

1897 — Frank Davenport's "Dig Ditch" brings irrigating water out of Hood River to lower west side. Land boom follows.

1903 — Japanese begin working in the Hood River region.

1906 — Mount Hood Railroad completed to Dee. Oregon Lumber Company sawmill and hotel built at Dee.

1907 — Yasui brothers arrive in Hood River and found store. Pioneer Society organized.

1908 — Hood River County established (formerly part of Wasco County).

1910 — Parkdale gets name. First store and post office (McIsaac's), hotel and Mount Hood Railroad terminus. Koberg's Beach established by Koberg family.

1913 — "Purely Cooperative" Apple Growers Association organized. Hood River Carnegie Library opens at present location.

1916 — Dedication of Columbia River Highway from Portland to Hood River.

(continued)

1917 — S.S. Bailey Gatzert leaves Columbia River, among last of sternwheelers to go.

1919 — December temperature is minus 27 degrees. Thousands of fruit trees killed. Pears replace many apple trees.

1921 — First annual American Legion Mount Hood Climb.

1924 — Interstate bridge at Hood River completed.

1926 — Loop Highway completed around Mount Hood. Crag Rats mountain rescue group organized.

1927 — Stone and concrete pavilion built at Koberg's Beach.

1935 — First Mexican family arrives in Upper Valley.

1937 — Columbia River freezes over (temperature drops to 12 degrees F).

1938 — Popular Koberg's Beach lost to waters behind new Bonneville Dam.

1946 — First annual Roy Webster cross channel swim (Labor Day).

1954 — Present county court house dedicated.

1967 — Highway 35 built.

1968 — I-84 (first known as I-80N) built.

1977 — Hood River County Historical Museum dedicated.

1980 — First windsurfing event held in the Gorge.

Hood River News Panorama, 1982, and
The History Museum of Hood River County

About The History Museum of Hood River County

The History Museum has been part of Hood River County since its very beginning in 1907 with the Pioneer Society and later the Historical Society. Its mission is to celebrate Hood River County's diverse cultural heritage and preserve its unique story. The museum has ongoing programs in education and community outreach that help keep the story alive and accessible for future generations. The museum is honored to have been the recipient of Ruth's wonderful collection of research notebooks and personal writing diaries. This collection will be preserved and shared, allowing us all a more intimate and personal look at our past.

For museum hours and details about its programs, go to www.co.hood-river.or.us/museum or call the museum office at 541-386-6772. This book, and many others that help highlight our local history, can be found in The History Shoppe located inside The History Museum.

A portion of the proceeds from each "Visits With Mrs. Picket" sold will go to The History Museum of Hood River County for ongoing archive and collection needs.

.

CPSIA information can be obtained
at www.ICGtesting.com
Printed in the USA
FSOW03n1101150317
31939FS